WORLD WAR II

WORLD WAR II

A Concise Military History
of America's All-Out,
Two-Front War

Adapted from
American Military History
Office of the Chief of Military History
United States Army

Maurice Matloff
General Editor

Galahad Books • New York City

Adapted from *American Military History*
Office of the Chief of Military History
United States Army

Maurice Matloff, General Editor

Portraits from Picture Collection,
The Branch Libraries, The New York Public Library

Published in 1982 by
Galahad Books
95 Madison Avenue
New York, NY 10016

Published by arrangement with David McKay Company, Inc.

Manufactured in the United States of America

10   9   8   7   6   5   4   3   2   1

Library of Congress Catalog Card Number 82-80326

ISBN 0-88365-617-5

CONTENTS

CHAPTER 1

Between World Wars

Soon after the armistice of November 1918 the War Department urged the Congress to authorize the establishment of a permanent Regular Army of nearly 600,000 and a three-month universal training system that would permit a quick expansion of this force to meet the requirements of a new major war. The Congress and American public opinion rejected these proposals. It was hard to believe that the defeat of Germany and the exhaustion of the other European powers did not guarantee that there would be no major war on land for years to come. Although the possibility of war with Japan was recognized, American leaders assumed that such a war, if it came, would be primarily naval in character. Indeed, the fundamental factor in the military policy of the United States during the next two decades was reliance on the United States Navy as the first line of national defense.

Another basic factor that determined the character of the Army between world wars was the decision of the United States not to join the League of Nations and therefore to reject participation in an active and co-operative world security system to maintain peace. The American people soon showed themselves unwilling to support an Army in being any larger than required to defend the continental United States and its overseas territories and possessions, to keep alive a knowledge of the military arts, and to train inexpensive and voluntary civilian components. Since the Army had huge stocks of

1

matériel left over from its belated production for World War I, the principal concern of the War Department until the 1930's was manpower to fulfill these peacetime missions.

Demobilization

Planning for demobilization had begun less than a month before the armistice, since few in the United States had expected the war to end so quickly. When the fighting in Europe stopped, almost all officers and men in the Army became eligible for discharge. The War Department had to decide how to muster out these men as rapidly and equitably as possible without unduly disrupting the national economy, while at the same time maintaining an effective force for occupation and other postwar duties. It decided in favor of the traditional method of demobilization by units as the one best calculated to achieve these ends. Units in the United States were moved to thirty demobilization centers located throughout the country, so that men after processing could be discharged near their homes. Units overseas were brought back just as rapidly as shipping space could be found for them, processed through debarkation centers operated by the Transportation Service, and then sent to the demobilization centers for discharge. In practice the unit system was supplemented by a great many individual discharges and by the release of certain occupational groups, notably railroad workers and anthracite coal miners.

In the first full month of demobilization the Army released about 650,000 officers and men, and within nine months it demobilized nearly 3,250,000 without seriously disturbing the American economy. A demobilization of war industry and disposal of surplus matériel paralleled the release of men, but the War Department kept a large reserve of weapons for peacetime or new emergency use. Despite the lack of much advance planning demobilization worked reasonably well. The Army was concerned at the outset because it had no authority to enlist men to replace those discharged. A law of February 28, 1919, permitted enlistments in the Regular Army for either one or three years; and by the end of the year the active Army, reduced to a strength of about 19,000 officers and 205,000 enlisted men, was again a Regular volunteer force.

2

Immediate Duties

At home during 1919 and 1920 Army forces continued the guard on the border of Mexico required by revolutionary disturbances in that country. Because of the lack of National Guard forces (not yet reorganized) the active Army until the summer of 1921 also had to supply troops on numerous occasions to help suppress domestic disorders, chiefly arising out of labor disputes and race conflicts in a restless postwar America.

Abroad, a newly activated United States Third Army moved into Germany on December 1, 1918, to occupy a segment of territory between Luxembourg and the Rhine River around Coblenz. As many as nine divisions participated in the German occupation during the spring of 1919. Similarly, an Army regiment sent to Italy before the end of hostilities participated for four months in the occupation of Austria. In Germany, American troops had no unusual difficulties with the populace, and soon after the peace conference ended in May 1919 the occupation forces were rapidly reduced. They numbered about 15,000 at the beginning of 1920. After rejecting the Treaty of Versailles the United States remained technically at war with Germany until the summer of 1921, when a separate peace was signed. Thereafter, the occupying force was gradually withdrawn, and the last thousand troops left for home on January 24, 1923.

Revolutionary turmoil in Soviet Russia induced President Wilson in August 1918 to direct Army participation in expeditions of United States and Allied forces that penetrated the Murmansk-Archangel region of European Russia and into Siberia via Vladivostock. The north Russian force, containing about 5,000 American troops under British command, suffered heavy casualties while guarding war supplies and communication lines before being withdrawn in June 1919. The Siberian force of about 10,000 under Maj. Gen. William S. Graves had many trying experiences in attempting to rescue Czech troops and in curbing Japanese expansionist tendencies between August 1918 and April 1920. Together these two forces incurred about as many combat casualties as the Army expeditionary force of similar size had sustained in Cuba in 1898. After the withdrawals from Germany and Russia, the only

3

Army forces stationed on foreign soil until 1941 were the garrison of about 1,000 maintained at Tientsin, China, from 1912 until 1938, and a force of similar strength dispatched from the Philippines to Shanghai for five months' duty in 1932. The Marine Corps rather than the Army provided the other small foreign garrisons and expeditionary forces required after World War I, particularly in the Caribbean area.

Reorganization Under the National Defense Act of 1920

After many months of careful consideration, Congress passed a sweeping amendment of the National Defense Act of 1916. The new National Defense Act of June 4, 1920, which governed the organization and regulation of the Army until 1950, has been widely acknowledged to be one of the most constructive pieces of military legislation ever adopted in the United States. It rejected the theory of an expansible Regular Army urged by Army leaders since the days of John C. Calhoun. Instead, it established the Army of the United States as an organization of three components, the professional Regular Army, the civilian National Guard, and the civilian Organized Reserves (Officers' and Enlisted Reserve Corps). Each component was to be so regulated in peacetime that it could contribute its appropriate share of troops in a war emergency. In effect the act acknowledged the actual practice of the United States throughout its history of maintaining a standing peacetime force too small to be expanded to meet the needs of a great war, and therefore necessarily of depending on a new Army of civilian soldiers for large mobilizations. In contrast to earlier practice, the training of civilian components now became a major peacetime task of the Regular Army, and principally for this reason the Army has authorized a maximum officer strength of 17,726 — more than three times the actual officer strength of the Regular Army before World War I. At least half of the new permanent officers were to be chosen from among non-Regulars who had served during the war. The act also provided that officer promotions, except for doctors and chaplains, were henceforth to be made from a single list, a step that equalized opportunity for advancement throughout most of the Army. The Regular Army was authorized a maximum enlisted strength of

280,000, but the actual enlisted as well as officer strength would depend on the amount of money voted in annual appropriations.

The new defense act also authorized the Army to continue all of its arm and service branches established before 1917, and to add three new branches, the Air Service, the Chemical Warfare Service, and a Finance Department, the first two reflecting new combat techniques demonstrated in the late war. The Tank Corps of World War I, representing another new technique, was absorbed by the Infantry. The act specifically charged the War Department with mobilization planning and preparation for the event of war. It assigned the military aspects of this responsibility to the Chief of Staff and the General Staff and the planning and supervision of industrial procurement to the Assistant Secretary of War.

World War I experience both in Washington and in France had greatly strengthened the position and authority of the General Staff. When General Pershing became Chief of Staff in 1921 he reorganized the War Department General Staff on the model of his wartime General Headquarters staff in France, to include five divisions: G-1 dealing with personnel, G-2 with intelligence, G-3 with training and operations, G-4 with supply, and a new War Plans Division that dealt with strategic planning and related preparations for the event of war. It was the War Plans Division that helped to draft "color" plans for the event of war with individual nations (as ORANGE, for war with Japan), and it was also planned that the staff of the War Plans Division would provide the nucleus for any new wartime General Headquarters established to direct operations. The General Staff divisions assisted the Chief of Staff in his supervision of the military branches of the War Department and of the field forces. The principal organizational change thereafter in the 1920's came in 1926 with the establishment of the Air Corps as an equal combat arm and with provision for its enlargement and modernization.

The field forces in the continental United States were put under the command and administration of nine corps areas approximately equal in population, and those overseas in Panama, Hawaii, and the Philippines under departments with similar authority. The division rather than the regiment became the basic Army unit, especially in mobilization planning, and each corps area was allocated 6 infantry divisions — 1 Regular Army, 2 National Guard, and 3

5

Reserve. In addition, a cavalry division patrolled the Mexican border, and in Pacific outposts Army mobile units were organized as separate Hawaiian and Philippine Divisions. The defense act had contemplated a higher organization of divisions into corps and armies, but no such tactical organizations existed in fact for many years.

Education for and within the Army between world wars received far greater attention than ever before. This situation reflected the emphasis in the National Defense Act on preparedness in peacetime as well as the increasing complexity of modern war. The United States Military Academy and the Reserve Officers' Training Corps program furnished most of the basic schooling for new officers. Thirty-one special service schools provided branch training. These branch schools trained officers and enlisted men of the civilian components besides those of the Regular Army, and furnished training through extension courses as well as on location. Three general service schools provided the capstone of the Army educational system. The oldest, located at Fort Leavenworth, Kansas, and known after 1928 as the Command and General Staff School, provided officers with the requisite training for divisional command and General Staff positions. In Washington the Army War College and, after 1924, the Army Industrial College trained senior officers of demonstrated ability for the most responsible command and staff positions. In establishing the Industrial College the Army recognized the high importance of logistical training for the conduct of modern warfare.

Regular Army Strength and Support

When the National Defense Act was adopted in June 1920, the Regular Army numbered about 200,000 — about two-thirds the maximum strength authorized in the act. In January 1921 Congress directed a reduction in enlisted strength to 175,000, and in June 1921 to 150,000, as soon as possible. A year later Congress limited the active Army to 12,000 commissioned officers and 125,000 enlisted men, not including the 7,000 or so in the Philippine Scouts, and Regular Army strength was stabilized at about this level until 1936. Appropriations for the military expenses of the War Department also became stabilized during this same period, amounting to about $300 million a year. This was about half of what a full implementation of the National Defense Act had been estimated to cost. The United States during these years spent rather less on its Army than on its Navy, in line with the national policy of depending on the Navy as the first line of defense. War Department officials, especially in the early 1920's, repeatedly expressed alarm over the failure of Congress to appropriate enough money to carry out the terms of the National Defense Act. They believed that it was essential for minimum defense needs to have a Regular Army with an enlisted strength of 150,000 or (after the Air Corps Act of 1926) of 165,000. As Chief of Staff Douglas MacArthur pointed out in 1933, the United States ranked seventeenth among the nations in active Army strength; but foreign observers rated its newly equipped Army Air Corps second or third in actual power.

In equipment the Air Corps offered a marked contrast to the rest of the Army. For almost two decades ground units had to get along as best they could with weapons left over from World War I. The Army was well aware that these old weapons were becoming increasingly obsolete, and that new ones were needed. For example, General MacArthur in 1933 described the Army's tanks (except for a dozen experimental models) as completely useless for employment against any modern unit on the battlefield. Although handicapped by very small appropriations for research and development, Army arsenals and laboratories worked continuously during the 1920's and 1930's to devise new items of equipment and to improve old ones. Service boards, links between branch schools and headquarters, tested pilot models and determined the doctrine for their employment so that it could be incorporated in training manuals. But not much new equipment was forthcoming for ground units in the field until Army appropriations began to rise in 1936.

For a number of years only about one-fourth of the officers and one-half of the enlisted men of the Regular Army were available for assignment to tactical units in the continental United States. Many units existed only on paper; almost all had only skeletonized strength. Instead of nine infantry divisions, there were actually three. In May 1927 one of these divisions, a cavalry brigade, and 200 planes participated in a combined arms maneuver in Texas, but for the most part Regular units had to train as battalions or companies. The continued dispersion of skeletonized divisions, brigades, and regiments among a large number of posts, many of them relics of the Indian wars, was a serious hindrance to the training of Regulars, although helpful in training the civilian components. Efforts to abandon small posts continued to meet with stubborn opposition from local interests and their elected representatives in Congress. In the infantry, for example, in 1932 the 24 regiments available in the United States for field service were spread among 45 posts, with a battalion or less at 34. Most of the organic transportation of these units was of World War I vintage, and the Army did not have the money to concentrate them for training by other means. Nor were there large posts in which they could be housed. The best training of larger units occurred overseas in the fairly sizable garrisons maintained by the Army in Hawaii, the Philippines, and Panama. In the early 1930's the great depression had the immediate effect of cuts in appropriations and pay that further reduced the readiness of Army units for military service.

Civilian Components

One of the major purposes of the National Defense Act had been to promote the integration of the Regular Army and the civilian components by establishing uniformity in training and professional standards. While in practice this purpose fell considerably short of full realization, nevertheless the new Army system saw an unprecedented amount of civilian military training. This training brought the Regular out of his traditional isolation from the civilian community, and it acquainted large numbers of civilians with the problems and views of the professional soldier. All together, the civilian components and the groups in training that contributed to their ranks had an average strength of about 400,000 between the wars. The end result of the civilian training program was to be an orderly and effective mobilization of National Guard and Reserve elements into the active Army in 1940 and 1941.

The absorption of the National Guard into the Army during World War I had left the states without any Guard units after the armistice. The act of 1920 contemplated a National Guard of 436,000, but its actual peacetime strength became stabilized at about 180,000. This force relieved the Regular Army of any duty in curbing domestic disturbances within the states from 1921 until 1941, and stood ready for immediate induction into the active Army whenever necessary. The War Department, in addition to supplying Regular officers for instruction and large quantities of surplus World War I matériel for equipment, applied about one-tenth of its military budget to the support of the Guard in the years between wars. Guardsmen engaged in 48 armory drills and 15 days of field training each year. Though not comparable to active Army units in readiness for war, the increasingly federalized Guard was better trained in 1939 than it had been when mobilized for Mexican border duty in 1916. Numerically, the National Guard was the largest component of the Army of the United States between 1922 and 1939.

In addition to the Guard, the civilian community had of course a very large number of trained officers and enlisted men after World War I, which assured the nation of a natural reservoir of manpower for the Army for a decade or more after the war. Only a very few of these men joined the Enlisted Reserve Corps, but large numbers of officers maintained their commissions in the Officers' Reserve Corps through five-year periods during which they received further training through school and extension courses and in brief tours of active duty. The composition of the Officers Reserve Corps, which numbered about 100,000 between the wars, gradually changed as its ranks were refilled by men newly commissioned after training in the Reserve Officers' Training Corps (ROTC) or the Citizens' Military Training Camp (CMTC) programs.

The ROTC program began long before the passage of the National Defense Act, in military colleges of which the first was Norwich University, established in 1819, in state land-grant schools set up under the Morrill Act of 1862, and in a number of private colleges and universities. For several decades before World War I the Army detailed annually up to 100 Regular officers as instructors, and supplied equipment, for college military training; but until the defense acts of 1916 and 1920 the program was only loosely associated with the Army's own needs. The new dependence on the civilian components for Army expansion, and the establishment of the Officers' Reserve Corps as a vehicle to retain college men in the Army of the United States after graduation, gave impetus to a

9

greatly enlarged and better regulated ROTC program after 1920. By 1928 there were ROTC units in 325 schools, about 225 of them being senior units enrolling 85,000 students in colleges and universities. Regular Army officers detailed as professors of military science instructed these units, and about 6,000 men graduating from them were commissioned each year in the Officers' Reserve Corps. This inexpensive program paid rich dividends when the nation again mobilized to meet the threat of war in 1940 and 1941.

The Army's CMTC program, a very modest alternative to the system of universal military training proposed in 1919, provided about 30,000 young volunteers with four weeks of military training in summer camps each year. Those who completed four years of CMTC training became eligible for Reserve commissions, the CMTC thus providing another (though much smaller) source for the rolls of the Officers' Reserve Corps and the National Guard.

Domestic Employment

The most notable domestic use of Regular troops in twenty years of peace happened in the nation's capital in the summer of 1932. Some thousands of "Bonus Marchers" remained in Washington after the adjournment of Congress dashed their hopes for immediate payment of a bonus for military service in World War I. On July 28, when marshals and police tried to evict one group encamped near the Capitol, a riot with some bloodshed occurred. Thereupon President Herbert C. Hoover called upon the Army to intervene. A force of about 600 — cavalrymen and infantrymen with a few tanks — advanced to the scene under the leadership of Chief of Staff MacArthur in person, two other generals, and, among junior officers, two whose names would in due course become much more familiar, Majors Dwight D. Eisenhower and George S. Patton, Jr. The troops cleaned up the situation near the Capitol without firing a shot, and then proceeded with equal efficiency to clear out all of the marchers from the District of Columbia. From a military point of view the Army had performed an unpleasant task in exemplary fashion, and with only a few minor injuries to participants; but the use of military force against civilians, most of them veterans,

10

tarnished the Army's public image and helped to defeat the administration in the forthcoming election.

Aside from the bonus incident, the most conspicuous employment of the Army within the United States during these years of peace was in a variety of nonmilitary tasks that only the Army had the resources and the organization to tackle quickly. In floods and blizzards and hurricanes it was the Army that was first on the spot with cots, blankets, and food. In another direction, Army Engineers expanded their work on rivers and harbors for the improvement of navigation and flood control. For four months in 1934 the Air Corps, on orders from President Franklin D. Roosevelt, took over the carrying of air mail for the Post Office Department with somewhat tragic consequences, since the corps was wholly unprepared for such an undertaking.

The most important and immediately disruptive nonmilitary duty began in 1933, after Congress passed an act that put large numbers of jobless young men into reforestation and other reclamation work. President Roosevelt directed the Army to mobilize these men and thereafter to run their camps without in any way making the Civilian Conservation Corps (CCC) program a military project in disguise. Within seven weeks the Army mobilized 310,000 men into 1,315 camps, a mobilization more rapid and orderly than any in the Army's history. For more than a year the War Department had to keep about 3,000 Regular officers and many noncommissioned officers assigned to this task, and in order to do so the Army had to strip tactical units of their leadership. Unit training was brought to a standstill, and the readiness of units for immediate military employment was almost destroyed. In the second half of 1934 the War Department called a large number of Reserve officers to active duty to replace the Regulars, and, by August 1935, 9,300 Reserve officers (not counted in active Army strength) were serving with the CCC. A good many of them continued in this service until 1941, but the Army never wanted to insert military training into the program, in part because the CCC camps were so small and so isolated. Despite its initial and serious interference with normal Army operations, in the long run the CCC program had a beneficial effect on military preparedness. It furnished many thousands of Reserve officers with valuable training, and it gave nonmilitary but

11

disciplined training to many hundreds of thousands of young men who were to become soldiers and sailors in World War II.

National and Military Policy

For fifteen years, from 1921 to 1936, the American people, their representatives in Congress, and their Presidents thought that the United States could and should avoid future wars with other major powers, except possibly Japan. They believed the nation could achieve this goal by maintaining a minimum of defensive military strength, avoiding entangling commitments with Old World nations, and yet using American good offices to promote international peace and the limitation of armaments. The United States took the initiative in 1921 in calling a conference in Washington to consider the limitation of armaments. The resulting naval treaty of 1922 temporarily checked a race for naval supremacy. It froze capital ship strengths of the United States, Great Britain, and Japan in a 5-5-3 ratio for a number of years. This ratio and restrictions on new naval base construction assured that neither the United States nor Japan could operate offensively in the Pacific as long as treaty provisions were respected. In effect these provisions also meant that it would be impossible for the United States to defend the Philippines against a Japanese attack. On the other hand, a general agreement among the western nations and Japan to maintain the *status quo* in the Pacific and in China offered fair assurance against a Japanese war of aggression, but only as long as the western powers did not themselves become embroiled in the European-Atlantic area.

In 1928 the United States and France joined in drafting the Pact of Paris, which renounced war as an instrument of national policy. Thereafter, the United States announced to the world that, if other powers did likewise, it would limit its armed forces to those necessary to maintain internal order and defend national territory against aggression and invasion. In 1931 the chief of the Army's War Plans Division advised the Chief of Staff that the defense of frontiers was precisely the cardinal task for which the Army had been organized, equipped, and trained. There was no real conflict between national policy and the Army's conception of its mission during the 1920's

12

and early 1930's. But in the Army's opinion the government and the American public, in their antipathy to war, failed to support even minimum needs for national defense.

Across the oceans, the clouds of war began to form again in 1931 when the Japanese seized Manchuria and then defied the diplomatic efforts of the League of Nations and the United States to pry them loose. In 1933 Japan quit the League and a year later announced that it would no longer be bound by the naval limitation treaties after they expired in 1936. In Europe, Adolf Hitler came to power in Germany in 1933, and by 1936 Nazi Germany had denounced the Treaty of Versailles, embarked on rearmament, and occupied the demilitarized Rhineland. Hitler's partner in dictatorship, Italy's Benito Mussolini, began his career of aggression by attacking Ethiopia in 1935. A revolution in Spain in 1936 not only produced a third dictatorship but also an extended war that became a proving ground for World War II. The neutrality acts passed by the Congress between 1935 and 1937 were a direct response to these European developments, and the United States tried to mend its international position in other ways by opening diplomatic relations with Soviet Russia in 1933, by promising eventual independence to the Philippines in 1934, and by liquidating its protectorates in the Caribbean area and pursuing the policy of the Good Neighbor toward Latin America generally.

No quick changes in American military policy followed. But beginning in 1935 the armed forces received substantially larger appropriations that permitted them to improve their readiness for action. Army improvements during the next three years reflected not only the increasingly critical international situation but also the careful planning of the War Department during General Douglas MacArthur's tour as Chief of Staff from 1930 to 1935. His recommendations led to a reorganization of the combat forces and a modest increase in their size, and were accompanied by more realistic planning for using the manpower and industrial might of the United States for war, if that should become necessary.

13

The Army Strengthened

The central objective of the Chief of Staff's recommendations had been to establish a small hard-hitting force ready for emergency use. In line with this objective the Army wanted to mechanize and motorize its Regular combat units as soon as it could, and to fill their ranks so that they could be trained effectively. The Army also needed new organizations to control training of the larger ground and air units and teams of combined arms in peacetime and to command them if war came. For these purposes the War Department between 1932 and 1935 created four army headquarters and a General Headquarters Air Force in the continental United States under command of the Chief of Staff. Under these headquarters, beginning in the summer of 1935, Regular and National Guard divisions and other units trained together each year in summer maneuvers and other exercises, including joint exercises with the Navy. In the same year Congress authorized the Regular Army to increase its enlisted strength to the long-sought goal of 165,000. This increase was accompanied during the following years by substantially greater expenditures for equipment and housing, so that by 1938 the Regular Army was considerably stronger and far readier for action than it had been in the early 1930's. But in the meantime the strength and power of foreign armies had been increasing even more rapidly.

In the slow rebuilding of the 1930's, the Army concentrated on equipping and training its combat units for mobile warfare rather than for the static warfare that had characterized operations on the Western Front in World War I. Through research it managed to acquire some new weapons that promised increased firepower and mobility as soon as equipment could be produced in quantity. In 1936 the Army adopted the Garand semiautomatic rifle to replace the 1903 Springfield, and during the 1930's it perfected the mobile 105-mm. howitzer that became the principal divisional artillery piece of World War II and developed light and medium tanks that were much faster than the lumbering models of World War I. In units, horse power gave way to motor power as rapidly as new vehicles could be acquired. To increase the maneuverability of its principal ground unit, the division, the Army decided after field tests to triangularize the infantry division by reducing the number of its infantry regiments from four to three, and to make it more mobile by using motor transportation only. The planned wartime strength of the new division was to be little more than half the size of its World War I counterpart.

Modern war is so complex and modern armies are so demanding in equipment that industrial mobilization for war must precede the large-scale employment of manpower by at least two years if a war is to be fought effectively. The Army's Industrial Mobilization Plan of 1930 established the basic principles for harnessing the nation's economic strength to war needs, and revisions of this plan to 1939 improved the pattern. Manpower planning culminated in the Protective Mobilization Plan of 1937. Under this plan the first step was to be the induction of the National Guard, to provide with the Regular Army an Initial Protective Force of about 400,000. The Navy and this defensive force would then protect the nation while the Army engaged in an orderly expansion to planned strengths of one, two, and four million, as necessary. Along with manpower planning there evolved for the first time prior to actual war a definite training plan, which included the location, size, and scheduling for replacement training centers, unit training centers, and schools, detailed unit and individual training programs, and the production of a variety of training manuals. While these plans were to help guide the mobilization that began in the summer of 1940, they had their faults. As it turned out the planners set their sights too low. They assumed a maximum mobilization of World War I dimension, whereas World War II was to call forth more than twice as many men and proportionately an even greater industrial effort for the Army. The plans also assumed until 1939 that mobilization for war would come more or less suddenly, instead of relatively slowly during many months of nominal peace.

The Beginnings of World War II

The German annexation of Austria in March 1938 followed by the Czech crisis in September of the same year awakened the United States and the other democratic nations to the imminence of another great world conflict. The new conflict had already begun in the Far

15

East when Japan had invaded China in 1937. After Germany seized Czechoslovakia in March 1939, war in Europe became inevitable, since Hitler had no intention of stopping with that move and Great Britain and France for their part decided that they must fight rather than yield anything more to Hitler. In August Germany made a deal with the Soviet Union, which provided for a partition of Poland and a Soviet free hand in Finland and the northern Baltic states. Then on September 1, 1939, Germany invaded Poland. When France and Great Britain responded by declaring war on Germany, they embarked on a course that could not lead to victory without aid from the United States. Yet an overwhelming majority of the American people wanted to stay out of the new war if they could, and this sentiment necessarily governed the initial responses of the United States Government and of its armed forces to the perilous international situation.

President Roosevelt and his advisers, being fully aware of the danger, had launched the nation on a limited preparedness campaign at the beginning of 1939. By then the technological improvement of the airplane had introduced a new factor into the military calculations of the United States. The moment was approaching when it would be feasible for a hostile Old World power to establish air bases in the Western Hemisphere from which the Panama Canal — then the key to American naval defense — or the continental United States itself might be attacked. Such a development would destroy the oceanic security that the American nation had so long enjoyed. The primary emphasis in 1939 was therefore on increasing the striking power of the Army Air Corps. At the same time Army and Navy officers collaborated in drafting the RAINBOW plans that superseded existing color plans and thereafter helped to guide the development and conduct of the American armed forces toward the war. A month after the European war began the President, in formally approving the RAINBOW I plan, changed the avowed national military policy from one of guarding the United States and its possessions only to one of hemisphere defense, and the policy of hemisphere defense was to be the focus of Army plans and actions until the end of 1940.

Immediately after the European war started the President proclaimed a limited national emergency and authorized increases in Regular Army and National Guard enlisted strengths to 227,000 and 235,000, respectively. He also proclaimed American neutrality in the war, but at his urging Congress presently gave indirect support to the western democracies by ending the prohibition on munitions sales to nations at war embodied in the Neutrality Act of 1937. British and French orders for munitions in turn helped to prepare American industry for the large-scale war production that was to come. When the quick destruction of Poland was followed by a lull in the war, the tempo of America's own defense preparations slackened. The Army concentrated on making its Regular force ready for emergency action by providing it with full and modern equipment as quickly as possible, and in April 1940 by engaging 70,000 troops in the first genuine corps and army training maneuvers in American military history. How adequate the Army was depended on the survival of France and Great Britain. The successful German seizure of Denmark and Norway in April 1940 followed by the quick defeat of the Low Countries and France and the grave threat to Great Britain forced the United States in June to adopt a new and greatly enlarged program for defense, for it then looked as if the nation might eventually have to face the aggressors of the Old World almost alone.

The Prewar Mobilization

Under the leadership of Chief of Staff General George C. Marshall and, after July, of Secretary of War Henry L. Stimson, the Army embarked in the summer of 1940 on a large expansion designed to protect the United States and the rest of the Western Hemisphere against any hostile forces that might be unleashed from the Old World. Army expansion was matched by a naval program designed to give the United States a two-ocean Navy strong enough to deal simultaneously with the Japanese in the Pacific and the naval strength that Germany and its new war partner, Italy, might acquire in the Atlantic if they defeated Great Britain. Both expansion programs had the overwhelming support of the American people, who though still strongly opposed to entering the war were now convinced that the danger to the United States was very real. Congressional appropriations between May and October 1940 reflected this conviction. The Army received more than $8 billion

17

GENERAL MARSHALL

for its needs during the succeeding year — a sum greater than what had been granted for the support of its military activities during the preceding twenty years. The munitions program approved for the Army on June 30, 1940, called for procurement by October 1941 of all items needed to equip and maintain a 1,200,000-man force, including a greatly enlarged and modernized Army Air Corps, and by September the War Department was planning to create an Army of a million and a half as soon as possible.

To fill the ranks of this new Army, Congress on August 27 approved induction of the National Guard into federal service and the calling up of the Organized Reserves. Then it approved the first peacetime draft of untrained civilian manpower in the nation's history, in the Selective Service and Training Act of September 14, 1940. Units of the National Guard, and selectees and the Reserve officers to train them, entered service as rapidly as the Army could construct camps to house them. During the last six months of 1940 the active Army more than doubled in strength, and by mid-1941 it achieved its planned strength of one and a half million officers and men.

18

A new organization, General Headquarters, took charge of training the Army in July 1940. In the same month the Army established a separate Armored Force, and subsequently Antiaircraft and Tank Destroyer Commands, which, with the Infantry, Field Artillery, Coast Artillery, and Cavalry, broadened the front of ground combat arms to seven. The existing branch schools and a new Armored Force School concentrated during 1940 and 1941 on improving the fitness of National Guard and Reserve officers for active duty, and in early 1941 the War Department established officer candidate schools to train men selected from the ranks for junior leadership positions. In October 1940 the four armies assumed command of ground units in the continental United States, and thereafter trained them under the supervision of General Headquarters. The corps area commands became administrative and service organizations. Major overseas garrisons were strengthened, and the Army established new commands to supervise the garrisoning of Puerto Rico and Alaska where there had been almost no Regular Army troops for many years. In June 1941 the War Department established the Army Air Forces to train and administer air units in the United States. In July it began the transformation of General Headquarters into an operational post for General Marshall as Commanding General of the Field Forces. By the autumn of 1941 the Army had 27 infantry, 5 armored, and 2 cavalry divisions, 35 air groups, and a host of supporting units in training in the continental United States. But most of these units were still unready for action, in part because the United States had shared so much of its old and new military equipment with the nations that were actively fighting the Axis triumvirate of Germany, Italy, and Japan.

Toward War

On the eve of France's defeat in June 1940 President Roosevelt had directed the transfer or diversion of large stocks of Army World War I weapons, and of ammunition and aircraft, to both France and Great Britain, and after France fell these munitions helped to replace Britain's losses in the evacuation of its expeditionary force from Dunkerque. More aid to Britain was forthcoming in September when the United States agreed to exchange fifty over-age destroyers for offshore Atlantic bases, and the President announced that henceforth production of heavy bombers would be shared equally with the British. An open collaboration with Canada from August 1940 onward led to a strong support of the Canadian war effort, Canada having followed Great Britain into war in September 1939. The foreign aid program culminated in the Lend-Lease Act of March 1941, which swept away the pretense of American neutrality by openly avowing the intention of the United States to become an "arsenal of democracy" against aggression. Prewar foreign aid was nonetheless a measure of self defense; its fundamental purpose was to help contain the military might of the Axis powers until the United States could complete its own protective mobilization.

Thus by early 1941 the focus of American policy had shifted from hemisphere defense to a limited participation in the war. Indeed by then it appeared to Army and Navy leaders and to President Roosevelt that the United States might be drawn into full participation in the not too distant future. Assuming the probability of simultaneous operations in the Pacific and Atlantic, they agreed that Germany was the greater menace and that if the United States did enter the war it ought to concentrate on the defeat of Germany first. This principle was accepted in staff conversations between American and British military representatives in Washington ending on March 29, 1941.

After these conversations the Army and Navy adjusted the most comprehensive of the prewar planning concepts, RAINBOW 5, to accord with American military preparations and actions during the remaining months of 1941 before the Japanese attack. During these months the trend was steadily toward American participation in the war against Germany. In April the President authorized an active naval patrol of the western half of the Atlantic Ocean. In May the United States decided to accept responsibility for the development and operation of military air routes across the North Atlantic via Greenland and across the South Atlantic via Brazil. During May it also appeared to the President and his military advisers that a German drive through Spain and Portugal to northwestern Africa and its adjacent islands might be imminent. This prospect together with German naval activity in the North Atlantic led the President to proclaim an unlimited national emergency, and to direct the

Army and Navy to prepare an expeditionary force to be sent to the Azores as a step toward blocking a German advance toward the South Atlantic. Then, in early June, the President learned that Hitler was preparing to attack the Soviet Union, a move that would divert German military power away from the Atlantic, at least for the time being.

The Germans invaded the Soviet Union on June 22, and three days later Army troops landed in Greenland to protect it against German attack and to build air bases for the air ferry route across the North Atlantic. Earlier in June the President had also decided that Americans should relieve British troops guarding Iceland, and the initial contingent of American forces reached there in early July, to be followed by a sizable Army expeditionary force in September. In August the President and British Prime Minister Winston Churchill met in Newfoundland and drafted the Atlantic Charter, which defined the general terms of a just peace for the world. By October the United States Navy was fully engaged in convoy-escort duties in the western reaches of the North Atlantic, and Navy ships, with some assistance from Army aircraft, were joining with British and Canadian forces in warring against German submarines. In November Congress voted to repeal prohibitions against the arming of American merchant vessels and their entry into combat zones, and the stage was set, as Prime Minister Churchill noted on November 9, for "constant fighting in the Atlantic between German and American ships."

Apparently all of the overt American moves in 1941 toward involvement in the war against Germany had solid backing in American public opinion, with only an increasingly small though vociferous minority criticizing the President for the nation's departures from neutrality. But the American people were still not prepared for an open declaration of war.

As the United States moved toward war in the Atlantic area, American policy toward Japan also stiffened. Although the United States wanted to avoid a two-front war, it was not ready to do so by surrendering vital areas or interests to the Japanese as the price of peace. When in late July 1941 the Japanese moved large forces into what became South Vietnam, the United States responded by freezing Japanese assets and cutting off oil shipments to Japan. At the same time the War Department recalled General MacArthur to active duty to command both United States and Philippine Army forces in the Far East and it also decided to send Army reinforcements to the Philippines, including heavy bombers intended to dissuade the Japanese from making any more southward moves. For their part the Japanese, while continuing to negotiate with the United States, tentatively decided in September to embark on a war of conquest in Southeast Asia and the Indies as soon as possible, and to try to immobilize American naval opposition by an opening air strike against the great American naval base of Pearl Harbor in Hawaii. When intensive last-minute negotiations in November failed to produce any accommodation, the Japanese made their decision for war irrevocable.

The Japanese attack of December 7, 1941 on Pearl Harbor and the Philippines at once ended the division of American opinion toward participation in the war, and America went to war with a unanimity of popular support that was unprecedented in the military history of the United States. This was also the first time in its history that the United States had entered a war with a large Army in being and an industrial system partially retooled for war. The Army numbered 1,643,477, and it was ready to defend the Western Hemisphere against invasion. But it was not ready to take part in large-scale operations across the oceans. Many months would pass before the United States could launch even limited offensives.

CHAPTER 2

World War II: The Defensive Phase

About one o'clock in Washington on the afternoon of December 7, 1941, the first news of the Japanese attack on Pearl Harbor, Hawaii, reached the War Department. The news came as a shock, even as the attack itself had come. It caught by surprise not only the American people at large, who learned of the attack a short while later, but also their leaders, including the very officers who had earlier been so much concerned over the possibility of just such an attack. One explanation is that these officers and their political superiors were momentarily expecting the Japanese to use all their forces against weakly held British and Dutch positions in the Far East (and probably, but not certainly, against the Philippines). But without warning in the early morning of December 7, powerful carrier-borne air forces had smashed the U.S. Pacific Fleet at anchor in Pearl Harbor. The same day (December 8 in the Philippines), about noon, Formosa-based bombers caught the bulk of the U.S. Far East Air Force lined up on Clark and Iba fields not far from Manila in central Luzon and virtually destroyed it. For the second time within a quarter-century, Americans found themselves fully involved in a war they had not sought — this time in the first truly global conflict.

23

The Outbreak of War: Action and Reaction

The attack on Pearl Harbor was one of the most brilliant tactical feats of the war. From 6 carriers which had advanced undetected to a position 200 miles north of Oahu, some 350 aircraft came in through the morning mist, achieving complete tactical surprise. They bombed and strafed the neatly aligned Army planes on Hickam and Wheeler Fields, as well as Navy and Marine Corps aircraft, and they carefully singled out as targets major units of the Navy's battle force at anchor in the harbor. Fortunately, the fleet's 3 carriers were away at the time, and the attackers failed to hit the oil tanks and naval repair shops on shore. But the blow was devastating enough. About 170 aircraft were destroyed and 102 damaged, all 8 battleships were sunk or badly damaged, besides many other vessels, and total casualties came to about 3,400, including 2,402 service men and civilians killed. Japanese losses were about 49 aircraft and 5 midget submarines. In an astonishing achievement, the enemy managed to apply in one shattering operation a combination of the principles of surprise, objective, mass, security, and maneuver. In its larger strategic context, the Pearl Harbor attack also exemplifies the principles of the offensive and economy of force. The joint Congressional committee investigating the attack called it the "greatest military and naval disaster in our Nation's history."

These two attacks — on Pearl Harbor and on the Philippines — effectively crippled American striking power in the Pacific. The Philippines and other American possessions in the western Pacific were isolated, their loss a foregone conclusion. The Hawaiian Islands and Alaska lay open to invasion; the Panama Canal and the cities, factories, and shipyards of the west coast were vulnerable to raids from the sea and air. Months would pass before the United States could regain a capacity for even the most limited kind of offensive action against its oriental enemy. As Japanese forces moved swiftly southward against the Philippines, Malaya, and the Netherlands Indies, Japan's Axis partners, Germany and Italy, promptly declared war on the United States, thus ending the uncertainty as to whether the United States would become a full-fledged belligerent in the European war. For the first time in its history, the United States was embarked upon an all-out, two-front war.

Meanwhile Britain was battling to maintain its hold on the eastern Mediterranean region which lay athwart the historic lifeline to possessions and Commonwealth associates in the Far East. Late in 1940 small British forces based in Egypt gained important successes against Italian armies in Libya, and the Greeks in the winter of 1940-41 resoundingly defeated an invading Italian army and chased it back into Albania. But German armies quickly came to the aid of their Italian ally. In April 1941 the famous panzer divisions, supported by overwhelming air power, swept through the Balkans, crushing the Yugoslav and Greek armies, and a British expeditionary force hastily dispatched to aid the latter. The following month German airborne forces descended on the island of Crete and swamped British and Greek defenders in a spectacular, though costly, attack. In Libya a powerful German-Italian army under General Erwin Rommel drove the British back across the Egyptian border, isolating a large garrison in Tobruk and threatening the Nile Delta. Against these disasters Britain could count only the final expulsion of the Italians from the Red Sea area and of the Vichy French from Syria, the suppression of pro-German uprisings in Iraq, and the achievement of a precarious naval ascendancy in the eastern and western portions of the Mediterranean. During the remainder of 1941 the British gradually built up strength in eastern Libya, and late in the year they succeeded in relieving Tobruk and pushing Rommel back to his original starting point at El Agheila.

Since mid-1940 the military fortunes of the anti-Axis powers had declined as the European war expanded. Germany had crushed all its continental European opponents in the west, and then attempted to destroy Britain's air forces as a prelude to an invasion across the English Channel. In the air battles over Britain in August and September 1940 the Royal Air Force won a brilliant victory. But during the following winter and spring the warning threat of invasion had been replaced by the equally deadly and more persistent menace of economic strangulation. German aircraft pulverized Britain's ports and inland cities, while U-boats, surface raiders, and mines decimated shipping. By 1941 the imports on which the United Kingdom depended for existence had dwindled to less than two-thirds of their prewar volume, and the British people faced the prospect of ultimate starvation.

In June 1941, however, the storm center of the war had moved

25

elsewhere. Only slightly delayed by the conquest of the Balkans, Hitler on June 22, 1941, hurled German might against the Soviet Union, the only remaining power on the European continent capable of challenging his dominance. By early December, when the onset of winter and stiffening Soviet resistance finally brought the advance to a halt, the German armies had driven to the suburbs of Moscow, inflicted huge losses on the Red Army, and occupied a vast expanse of European Russia embracing its most densely populated and industrialized regions. This, as it turned out, was the high tide of German success in World War II; Hitler, like Napoleon, was to meet disaster on the wind-swept plains of Russia. But in December 1941 few were willing to predict this outcome. British and United States leaders assembling in Washington at the end of that month to make plans for dealing with the crisis had to reckon with the probability that in the year to come, unless the Western Allies could somehow force Germany to divert substantial forces from the eastern front, the German steamroller would complete the destruction of the Soviet armies. Hitler would then be able, with the resources and enslaved peoples of all Europe at his feet, to throw his full power against the West.

American military leaders had already given thought to this grim prospect, and to the implications it held for America's role in the war. In the Victory Program, drawn up by the Army and Navy at the President's behest during the summer of 1941, the leaders of the two services had set forth in some detail the strategy and the means they considered necessary to win ultimate victory if, as they expected, Soviet Russia succumbed to the Axis onslaught. The strategy was the one laid down in the RAINBOW 5 war plan — wear Germany down by bombing, blockade, subversion, and limited offensives, while mobilizing the strength needed to invade the European continent and to defeat Germany on its own ground. Japan meanwhile would be contained by air and sea power, local defense forces, China's inexhaustible manpower, and the Soviet Union's Siberian divisions. With Germany out of the running, Japan's defeat or collapse would soon follow. As for the means, the United States would have to provide them in large part, for the British were already weary and their resources limited. The United States would serve not merely, to use the President's catchy phrase, as the "arsenal of democracy," supplying weapons to arm its allies, but also as

26

the main source of the armies without which wars, above all this war, could not be won. Army leaders envisaged the eventual mobilization of 215 divisions, 61 of them armored, and 239 combat air groups, requiring a grand total, with supporting forces, of 8.8 million men. Five million of these would be hurled against the European Axis. It was emphasized that victory over the Axis Powers would require a maximum military effort and full mobilization of America's immense industrial resources.

Yet the Victory Program was merely an expression of professional military views, not a statement of national military policy. That policy, on the eve of Pearl Harbor, was still ostensibly hemisphere defense. The pace of rearmament and mobilization, in the summer and fall of 1941, was actually slowing down. Signs pointed to a policy of making the American contribution to the defeat of the Axis, as columnist Walter Lippmann put it, one "basically of Navy, Air, and manufacturing," something a great deal less than the all-out effort envisaged in the Victory Program. Public and Congressional sentiment, moreover, still clung to the hope that an immediate showdown with the Axis Powers could be avoided and that the country would not be forced into full belligerent participation in the war, as evidenced by a near defeat of the bill to extend Selective Service, continuation of a prohibition against sending selectees outside the Western Hemisphere, and apathetic public response to submarine attacks on American destroyers in September and October.

The Japanese attack on Pearl Harbor and the Philippines changed the picture. A wave of patriotic indignation over Japanese duplicity and brutality swept the country. Isolationism virtually evaporated as a public issue, and all parties closed ranks in support of the war effort. Indeed, in retrospect, despite the immediate tactical success the Japanese achieved at Pearl Harbor, that attack proved to be a great blunder for them, politically and strategically. The President, early in January, dramatized the magnitude of the effort now demanded by proclaiming a new set of production goals — 60,000 airplanes in 1942 and 125,000 in 1943; 45,000 tanks in 1942 and 75,000 in 1943; 20,000 antiaircraft guns in 1942 and 35,000 in 1943; half a million machine guns in 1942 and as many more in 1943; and 8 million deadweight tons of merchant shipping in 1942 and 10 million in 1943. Vanished were the two illusions

27

that America could serve only as an arsenal of democracy, contributing weapons without the men to wield them, or conversely, that the nation could rely solely on its own fighting forces, leaving other anti-Axis nations to shift for themselves. "We must not only provide munitions for our own fighting forces," Roosevelt advised Secretary of War Henry L. Stimson, "but vast quantities to be used against the enemy in every appropriate theater of war." A new Victory Program boosted the Army's ultimate mobilization goal to 10 million men, and the War Department planned to have 71 divisions and 115 combat air groups organized by the end of 1942, with a total of 3.6 million men under arms. As an Army planner had predicted back in the spring of 1941, the United States now seemed destined to become "the final reserve of the democracies both in manpower and munitions."

Late in December 1941 President Roosevelt and Prime Minister Churchill met with their advisers in Washington (the ARCADIA Conference) to establish the bases of coalition strategy and concert immediate measures to meet the military crisis. They faced an agonizing dilemma. Prompt steps had to be taken to stem the spreading tide of Japanese conquest. On the other hand, it seemed likely that the coming year might see the collapse of Soviet resistance and of the British position in the Middle East. In this difficult situation the Allied leaders made a far-reaching decision that shaped the whole course of the war. Reaffirming the principle laid down in Anglo-American staff conversations in Washington ten months earlier, they agreed that the first and main effort must go into defeating Germany, the more formidable enemy. Japan's turn would come later. Defeating Germany would involve a prolonged process of "closing and tightening the ring" about Fortress Europe. Operations in 1942 would have to be defensive and preparatory, though limited offensives might be undertaken if the opportunity offered. Not until 1943 at the earliest could the Allies contemplate a return to the European continent "across the Mediterranean, from Turkey into the Balkans, or by landings in Western Europe."

Another important action taken at the ARCADIA Conference was the establishment of the Combined Chiefs of Staff (CCS). This was a committee consisting of the professional military chiefs of both countries, responsible to the President and Prime Minister for planning and directing the grand strategy of the coalition. Its American members were the Army Chief of Staff, General Marshall; the Chief of Naval Operations, Admiral Harold R. Stark (replaced early in 1942 by Admiral Ernest J. King); and the Chief (later Commanding General) of the Army Air Forces, Lt. Gen. Henry H. Arnold. In July 1942 a fourth member was added, the President's personal Chief of Staff, Admiral William D. Leahy. Since the CCS normally sat in Washington, the British Chiefs of Staff, making up its British component, attended in person only at important conferences with the heads of state. In the intervals they were represented in Washington by the four senior members of the permanent British Joint Staff Mission, headed until late in 1944 by Field Marshal Sir John Dill, the former Chief of the British Imperial General Staff. Under the CCS a system of primarily military subordinate committees grew up, specifically designated to handle such matters as strategic and logistical planning, transportation, and communications.

By February 1942 the Joint Chiefs of Staff (JCS), consisting of the U.S. members of the CCS, had emerged as the highest authority in the U.S. military hierarchy (though never formally chartered as such), and responsible directly to the President. Like the CCS, the JCS in time developed a machinery of planning and working committees, the most important of which were the Joint Staff Planners, the Joint Strategic Survey Committee, and the Joint Logistics Committee. No executive machinery was created at either the CCS or JCS level. The CCS ordinarily named either the British Chiefs or the U.S. Joint Chiefs to act as its executive agent, and these, in turn, employed the established machinery of the service departments.

In the spring of 1942 Britain and the United States agreed on a worldwide division of strategic responsibility. The U.S. Joint Chiefs of Staff were to be primarily responsible for the war in the Pacific, and the British Chiefs for the Middle East-Indian Ocean region, while the European-Mediterranean-Atlantic area would be a combined responsibility of both staffs. China was designated a separate theater commanded by its chief of state, Chiang Kai-shek, though within the United States' sphere of responsibility. In the Pacific, the Joint Chiefs established two main theaters, the Southwest Pacific Area (SWPA) and the Pacific Ocean Areas (POA), the former under General MacArthur, the latter under Admiral Chester W. Nimitz. POA was further subdivided into

North, Central, and South Pacific areas, the first two directly controlled by Nimitz, the third by his deputy, Admiral William F. Halsey, Jr. (*See Map 2.*) Later in 1942, the U.S. air and service troops operating in China, India, and northern Burma were organized as U.S. Army Forces, China-Burma-India, under Lt. Gen. Joseph W. Stilwell. On various other far-flung lines of communications U.S. Army forces, mostly air and service troops during 1942, were organized under similar theater commands. In June Maj. Gen. Dwight D. Eisenhower arrived in England to take command of the newly established European Theater of Operations, and after the landings in North Africa late in the year a new U.S. theater was organized in that region.

The British and the Americans had decided at the ARCADIA Conference that Allied forces in each overseas theater would operate, as far as possible, under a single commander, and this principle was subsequently applied in most theaters. Within theaters subordinate unified commands were created, in some cases for Allied ground, naval, or air forces, and most frequently for task forces formed to carry out a specific operation or campaign. The authority of Allied theater commanders over national forces was always restricted with respect to areas and missions and, as a last resort, senior national commanders in each theater could appeal to their own governments against specific orders or policies of the theater commander. In practice, this right of appeal was rarely invoked.

In essence, unified command at the Allied level gave the commander control of certain specific forces for operational purposes, rather than jurisdiction over a given geographical area. Administration of national forces and the allocation of resources were usually handled through separate national channels. In certain cases, inter-Allied boards or committees, responsible to the Allied theater commander, controlled the common use of critical resources (such as petroleum products) or facilities (such as railways and shipping) within a theater. Administration of U.S. forces overseas also generally followed separate Army and Navy channels, except in the Pacific where, from 1943 on, supply, transportation, and certain other services were jointly administered to a limited degree.

Even before Pearl Harbor, Army leaders had realized that the peacetime organization of the War Department General Staff, dating back to 1921, was an inadequate instrument for directing a major war effort. Originally a small co-ordinating and planning body, the General Staff, and especially its War Plans and Supply Divisions, rapidly expanded during the emergency period into a large operating organization, increasingly immersed in the details of supervision to the detriment of its planning and policy-making functions. The Chief of Staff, to whom some sixty-one officers and agencies had direct access, carried an especially heavy burden.

Three additional features of the organization demanded remedy. One was the continued subordination of the Army Air Forces to General Staff supervision, which conflicted with the Air Forces' drive for autonomy. Another was the anomalous position of General Headquarters (GHQ), whose role as command post for the field forces and responsibilities in the fields of training and logistics clashed with the authority of the General Staff at many points. Finally, the division of supply responsibilities between the Supply Division (G-4) and the Office of the Under Secretary of War — with requirements and distribution assigned to the former and procurement to the latter — was breaking down under the pressure of mobilization.

Spurred by the Pearl Harbor disaster, which seemed to accentuate the need for better staff co-ordination in Washington, General Marshall on March 9, 1942, put into effect a sweeping reorganization of the War Department. Under the new plan, which underwent little change during the war years, the General Staff, except for the War Plans and Intelligence Divisions, was drastically whittled down and limited in function to broad planning and policy guidance. An expanded War Plans Division, soon renamed Operations Division (OPD), became General Marshall's command post and, in effect, a superior general staff for the direction of overseas operations. The Army Air Forces, though in some respects on a lower level of administrative authority than before, had virtually complete control of the development of its special weapon — the airplane. Administering its own personnel and training, it organized and supported the combat air forces to be employed in theaters of operations and came also to exercise considerable influence over both strategic and operational planning.

In the reorganization of March 9 two new commands were created, the Army Ground Forces (AGF) and the Services of Supply, later renamed the Army Service Forces (ASF). The former, headed by Lt. Gen. Lesley J. McNair, took over the training mission of GHQ, now abolished, and absorbed the ground combat arms. To the ASF, commanded by Lt. Gen. Brehon B. Somervell, were subordinated the supply (renamed technical) and administrative services, the nine corps areas, and most of the Army posts and installations throughout the United States, including the ports of embarkation through which troops and supplies flowed to the forces overseas. In supply matters, Somervell now reported to two masters, the Chief of Staff for requirements and distribution and the Under Secretary of War, Mr. Robert P. Patterson, for procurement. His subordination to the latter was, in reality, only nominal since most of Patterson's organization was transferred bodily to Somervell's headquarters. Except for equipment peculiar to the Army Air Forces, the ASF thus became the Army's central agency for supply in the United States. It drew up the Army's "shopping list" of requirements, the Army Supply Program; through the seven technical services (Quartermaster, Ordnance, Signal, Chemical, Engineer, Medical, and Transportation) it procured most of the Army's supplies and equipment; it distributed these materials to the Army at home and abroad, as well as to Allies under lend-lease; it operated the Army's fleet of transports; and it trained specialists and service units to perform various specialized jobs. General Somervell himself became General Marshall's principal logistical adviser.

All this looked to the future. In the first few weeks after Pearl Harbor, while the Navy was salvaging what it could from the wreckage at Pearl Harbor and striving to combat German submarines in the western Atlantic, the War Department made desperate efforts to bolster the defenses of Hawaii, the Philippines, the Panama Canal, Alaska, and the U.S. west coast. By the end of December, the danger of an attack on the Hawaii-Alaska-Panama triangle seemed to have waned, and the emphasis shifted to measures to stave off further disasters in the Far East. The British and Americans decided at ARCADIA that the Allies would attempt to hold the Japanese north and east of the line of the Malay Peninsula and the Netherlands Indies and to re-establish communications with the Philippines to the north. To co-ordinate operations in this vast theater, the Allied leaders created the ABDA (American-British-Dutch-Australian) Command, including the Netherlands Indies, Malaya, Burma, and the Philippines. British Lt. Gen. Sir

Archibald P. Wavell was placed in over-all command. Through India from the west and Australia from the east, the Allies hoped in a short time to build up a shield of air power stout enough to blunt the Japanese threat.

For a time it seemed as though nothing could stop the Japanese juggernaut. In less than three weeks after Pearl Harbor, the isolated American outposts of Wake and Guam fell to the invaders, the British garrison of Hong Kong was overwhelmed, and powerful land, sea, and air forces were converging on Malaya and the Netherlands Indies. Picked, jungle-trained troops drove down the Malay Peninsula toward the great fortress of Singapore, infiltrating and outflanking successive British positions. Two of the most formidable warships in the British Navy, the battleship *Prince of Wales* and the battle cruiser *Repulse,* were sunk by Japanese torpedo planes off the east coast of Malaya, a loss that destroyed the Allies' last hope of effectively opposing Japan's naval power in the Far East. Attacked from the land side, Singapore and its British force of over 80,000 troops surrendered on February 15, 1942. Meanwhile the Japanese had invaded the Netherlands Indies from the north, west, and east. In a series of actions during January and February, the weak Dutch and Australian naval forces, joined by the U.S. Asiatic Fleet withdrawing from the Philippines, were destroyed piecemeal, only four American destroyers escaping south to Australia. On March 9 the last Allied ground and air forces in the Netherlands Indies, almost 100,000 men (mostly Indonesian troops) surrendered to the invaders. In Burma, the day before, the British had been forced under heavy bombing to evacuate Rangoon and retreat northward. Before the end of April the Japanese had completed the occupation of Burma, driving the British westward into India and the bulk of U.S. Lt. Gen. Joseph W. Stilwell's Chinese forces back into China; General Stilwell and the remnants of other Chinese units retreated to India. In the process the Japanese had won possession of a huge section of the Burma Road, the only viable route between China and India. Henceforth and until late in the war communication between China and its allies was to be limited to an air ferry from India over the "hump" of the Himalayan Mountains. During the late spring strong Japanese naval forces reached the coastal cities of India and even attacked Britain's naval base on Ceylon.

By May 1942 the Japanese had thus gained control of Burma,

Malaya, Thailand, French Indochina, and the Malay Archipelago, while farther to the east they had won strong lodgments on the islands of New Guinea and New Britain and in the Solomons, flanking the approaches to Australia and New Zealand from the United States. This immense empire had been won at remarkably little cost through an effective combination of superior air and sea power and only a handful of well-trained ground divisions. The Japanese had seized and held the initiative while keeping their opponents off balance. They had concentrated their strength for the capture of key objectives such as airfields and road junctions and for the destruction of major enemy forces while diverting only minimum forces on secondary missions, thus giving an impression of overwhelming numerical strength. They had frequently gained the advantage of surprise and had baffled their enemies by their speed and skill in maneuver. The whole whirlwind campaign, in short, had provided Japan's enemies with a capsule course of instruction in the principles of war.

Fall of the Philippines

Only in the Philippines, almost on Japan's southern doorstep, was the timetable of conquest delayed. When the Japanese struck, the defending forces in the islands numbered more than 130,000, including the Philippine Army which, though mobilized to a strength of ten divisions, was ill trained and ill equipped. Of the U.S. Army contingent of 31,000, more than a third consisted of the Philippine Scouts, most of whom were part of the Regular Army Philippine Division, the core of the mobile defense forces. The Far East Air Force, before the Japanese attack, had a total of 277 aircraft of all types, mostly obsolescent but including 35 new heavy bombers. Admiral Thomas C. Hart's Asiatic Fleet, based on the Philippines, consisted of 3 cruisers, 13 old destroyers, 6 gunboats, 6 motor torpedo boats, 32 patrol bombers, and 29 submarines. A regiment of marines, withdrawn from Shanghai, also joined the defending forces late in November 1941. Before the end of December, however, American air and naval power in the Philippines had virtually ceased to exist. The handful of bombers surviving the early attacks had been evacuated to Australia, and the bulk of the Asiatic

Fleet, its base facilities in ruins, had withdrawn southward to help in the defense of the Netherlands Indies.

The main Japanese invasion of the Philippines, following preliminary landings, began on December 22, 1941. While numerically inferior to the defenders, the invading force of two divisions with supporting units was well trained and equipped and enjoyed complete mastery of the air and on the sea. The attack centered on Luzon, the northernmost and largest island of the archipelago, where all but a small fraction of the defending forces were concentrated. The main landings were made on the beaches of Lingayen Gulf, in the northwest, and Lamon Bay in the southeast. General MacArthur's plan was to meet and destroy the invaders on the beaches, but his troops were unable to prevent the enemy from gaining secure lodgments. On December 23 MacArthur ordered a general withdrawal into the mountainous Bataan Peninsula, across Manila Bay from the capital city. Manila itself was occupied by the Japanese without resistance. The retreat into Bataan was a complex operation, involving converging movements over difficult terrain into a cramped assembly area from which only two roads led into the peninsula itself. Under constant enemy attack, the maneuver was executed with consummate skill and at considerable cost to the attackers. Yet American and Filipino losses were heavy, and the unavoidable abandonment of large stocks of supplies foredoomed the defenders of Bataan to ultimate defeat in the siege that followed. An ominous portent was the cutting of food rations by half on the last day of the retreat.

By January 7, 1942, General MacArthur's forces held well-prepared positions across the upper part of the Bataan Peninsula. Their presence there, and on Corregidor and its satellite island fortresses guarding the entrance to Manila Bay, denied the enemy the use of the bay throughout the siege. In the first major enemy offensive, launched early in January, the "battling bastards of Bataan" at first gave ground but thereafter handled the Japanese so roughly that attacks ceased altogether from mid-February until April, while the enemy reorganized and heavily reinforced. The defenders were, however, too weak to seize the initiative themselves.

General MacArthur, meanwhile, was ordered by the President to leave his post and go to Australia in order to take command of Allied operations against the Japanese in the Southwest Pacific. In mid-

GENERAL WAINRIGHT BROADCASTING TO AMERICAN FORCES

March he and a small party made their way through the Japanese lines by motor torpedo boat to Mindanao, and from there were flown to Australia. Command of the forces in the Philippines devolved upon Lt. Gen. Jonathan M. Wainwright.

By April the troops on Bataan were subsisting on about fifteen ounces of food daily, less than a quarter of the peacetime ration. Their diet, consisting mostly of rice supplemented by carabao, mule, monkey, or lizard meat, was gravely deficient in vitamins and provided less than 1,000 calories a day, barely enough to sustain life. Weakened by hunger and poor diet, thousands succumbed to malaria, dengue, scurvy, beriberi, and amoebic dysentery, made impossible to control by the shortage of medical supplies, especially quinine. Desperate efforts were made to send food, medicine, ammunition, and other supplies through the Japanese blockade to the beleaguered forces. But during the early weeks, before the enemy cordon had tightened, it proved impossible, despite promises of lavish pay and bonuses, to muster the necessary ships and crews. Even so, sizable stocks were accumulated in the southern islands, but only about 1,000 tons of rations ever reached Manila Bay.

36

Shipments in converted destroyers from the United States were too late and too few, and only insignificant quantities could be brought in by submarine and aircraft.

At the beginning of April the Japanese, behind a pulverizing artillery barrage, attacked again. The American lines crumpled, and in a few days the defending forces virtually disintegrated. On April 9 Maj. Gen. Edward P. King, Jr., commanding the forces on Bataan, surrendered. For almost another month the garrison on Corregidor and the other islands, swelled by refugees from Bataan, held out under air bombardment and almost continuous plunging fire from heavy artillery massed on adjacent shores and heights — one of the most intense artillery bombardments, for so small a target, of the entire war. On the night of May 5, after a final terrific 5-day barrage, Japanese assault troops won a foothold on Corregidor, and the following night, when it became apparent that further resistance was useless, General Wainwright surrendered unconditionally. Under his orders, which the Japanese forced him to broadcast, other American commanders in the Philippines capitulated one by one. By early June, except for scattered guerrilla detachments in the hills, all organized resistance in the islands had ceased.

Deploying American Military Strength

After more than a year and a half of rearming, the United States in December 1941 was still in no position to carry the war to its enemies. On December 7 the Army numbered some 1,644,000 men (including about 120,000 officers), organized into 4 armies, 37 divisions (30 infantry, 5 armored, 2 cavalry), and over 40 combat air groups. Three of the divisions were overseas (2 in Hawaii, 1 in the Philippines), with other garrison forces totaling less than 200,000. By spreading equipment and ammunition thin, the War Department might have put a substantial force into the field to repel an attack on the continental United States; 17 of the divisions at home were rated as technically ready for combat. But these divisions lacked the supporting units and the training necessary to weld them into corps and armies. More serious still, they were inadequately equipped with many weapons that recent operations in Europe had shown to be indispensable — for example, tank and antitank guns,

37

antiaircraft artillery, radios, and radar — and some of these shortages were aggravated by lack of auxiliary equipment like fire control mechanisms.

Above all, ammunition of all kinds was so scarce that the War Department was unwilling to commit more than one division and a single antiaircraft regiment for service in any theater where combat operations seemed imminent. Only one division-size task force, in fact, was sent to the far Pacific before April 1942. Against air attacks, too, the country's defenses were meager. Along the Pacific coast the Army had only 45 modern fighter planes ready to fly, and only twelve 3-inch antiaircraft guns to defend the whole Los Angeles area. On the east coast there were only 54 Army fighter planes ready for action. While the coastal air forces, primarily training commands, could be reinforced by aircraft from the interior of the country, the total number of modern fighter aircraft available was less than 1,000. Fortunately, there was no real threat of an invasion in force, and the rapidly expanding output of munitions from American factories promised to remedy one of these weaknesses within a few months. Furthermore, temporary diversions of lend-lease equipment, especially aircraft, helped to bolster the overall defense posture within the first few weeks after Pearl Harbor. The Army hoped by April to have as many as thirteen divisions equipped and supplied with ammunition for combat.

To deploy these forces overseas was another matter. Although the U.S. merchant marine ranked second only to Great Britain's and the country possessed an immense shipbuilding capacity, the process of chartering, assembling, and preparing shipping for the movement of troops and military cargo took time. Time was also needed to schedule and organize convoys, and, owing to the desperate shortage of escort vessles, troop movements had to be widely spaced. Convoying and evasive routing, in themselves, greatly reduced the effective capacity of shipping. Moreover, vast distances separated U.S. ports from the areas threatened by Japan, and to these areas went the bulk of the forces deployed overseas during the months immediately following Pearl Harbor. Through March 1942, as a result, the outflow of troops to overseas bases averaged only about 50,000 per month, as compared with upwards of 250,000 during 1944, when shipping was fully mobilized and plentiful and the sea lanes were secure.

There seemed a real danger early in 1942, however, that German U-boats might succeed in reducing transatlantic deployment to a trickle — not so much by attacking troop transports, most of which could outrun their attackers, as by sinking the slow cargo ships on which the forces overseas depended for support. Soon after Germany's declaration of war, the U-boats struck at the virtually unprotected shipping lanes in the western Atlantic, and subsequently extended their attacks to the Gulf of Mexico and Caribbean areas and the mouth of the St. Lawrence. During the spring of 1942 tankers and freighters were torpedoed in plain view of vacationers on east coast beaches, and coastal cities dimmed or extinguished their lights in order that ships might not provide silhouetted targets for the U-boats. The Navy lacked the means to cope with the peril. In late December 1941 it had only twenty assorted surface vessels and about a hundred aircraft to protect the whole North Atlantic coastal frontier. During the winter and spring these were supplemented by another hundred Army planes of longer range, several armed British trawlers, and as many improvised craft as could be pressed into service.

But the toll of ship sinkings increased. In March 788,000 deadweight tons of Allied and neutral dry cargo shipping were lost, in June 936,000 tons. Tanker losses reached an all-time peak of 375,-000 tons in March, leading to complete suspension of coastal tanker movements and to gasoline rationing in the seaboard states. During the first six months of 1942 losses of Allied shipping were almost as heavy as during the whole of 1941 and exceeded new construction by almost 2.8 million deadweight tons. Although the United States was able by May to balance its own current losses by building new ships, Britain and other Allied countries continued until the following August to lose more than they could build, and another year passed before new construction offset cumulative losses.

Slowly and with many setbacks a system of countermeasures was developed. Convoying of coastal shipping, with ships sailing only by day, began in the spring of 1942. North-South traffic between U.S. and Caribbean and South American ports was also convoyed, on schedules interlocked with those of the transatlantic convoys. The latter, during 1942, were protected in the western half of the Atlantic by the U.S. and Canadian Navies, in the eastern half by the British. Troops were transported across the Atlantic either without escort in large, speedy liners like the *Queen Elizabeth* and the *Queen Mary* — which between them carried almost a quarter of all U.S. troops sent to Europe — or in heavily escorted convoys. Throughout the war, not a single loaded troop transport was sunk on the United Kingdom run. The slow merchant ships were convoyed in large groups according to speed.

But with responsibility for U.S. antisubmarine operations divided between the Navy and Army Air Forces, effective co-operation was hampered by sharp disagreement over organization and methods, and available resources throughout 1942 were inadequate. The U-boats, meanwhile, were operating with deadly effect and in growing numbers. Late in the year they began to hunt in packs, resupplied at sea by large cargo submarines ("milch cows"). The Allied convoys to Murmansk and other northern Soviet ports suffered especially heavy losses on their long passage around the top of the Scandinavian peninsula. In November shipping losses from all causes soared above 1.1 million deadweight tons — the peak, as it turned out, for the entire war, but few at the time dared so to predict.

In the Pacific, fortunately, the principal barriers to deployment of U.S. forces were distance and lack of prepared bases, not enemy submarines. Japan's fleet of undersea craft made little effort to prey on the Allied sea lanes and probably, over the vast reaches of the Pacific, could not have inflicted serious damage in any case. The chief goal of American deployment to the Pacific during most of 1942, following the initial reinforcement of Hawaii and the Panama Canal, was to build up a base in Australia and secure the chain of islands leading to it. Australia was a vast, thinly populated, and, except in its southeastern portion, largely undeveloped island continent, 7,000 miles and almost a month's sail from the U.S. west coast. It had provided a haven for some 4,000 American troops who, on December 7, had been at sea, bound for the Philippines, and in January a task force of division size (POPPY Force) was hastily assembled and dispatched to New Caledonia to guard its eastern approaches. During the first few weeks the main effort of the small American forces went into sending relief supplies to the Philippines and aircraft and troops to Java to stem the Japanese invasion. Beginning in March, as the futility of these efforts became evident, and coincident with the arrival of General MacArthur to assume command of all Allied forces in the Southwest Pacific, the construction of base facilities and the build-up of balanced air and ground forces got under way in earnest.

This build-up had as its first object the defense of Australia itself, for at the end of January the Japanese had occupied Rabaul on New Britain Island, thus posing an immediate threat to Port Moresby, the weakly held Australian base in southeastern New Guinea. In February President Roosevelt pledged American help in countering this threat, and in March and April two infantry divisions (the 41st and 32d) left the United States for the Southwest Pacific. At the same time, construction of air and refueling bases was being rushed to completion in the South Pacific islands that formed steppingstones along the ocean routes to Australia and New Zealand. After the western anchor of this chain, New Caledonia, was secured by the POPPY Force, Army and Marine garrisons and reinforcements were sent to various other islands along the line, culminating with the arrival of the 37th Division in the Fiji Islands in June.

These moves came none too soon for, during the spring, the Japanese, after occupying Rabaul, pushed into the southern Solomons, within easy striking distance of the American bases on Espíritu Santo and New Caledonia. They also occupied the northeastern coast of New Guinea, just across the narrow Papuan peninsula from Port Moresby, which the Americans and Australians were developing into a major advanced base in preparation for an eventual offensive northward. The stage was thus set for a major test of strength in the Pacific — American forces spread thinly along an immense arc from Hawaii to Australia, with outposts far to the north in Alaska; the Japanese securely in possession of the vast areas north and west of the arc and, with the advantage of interior lines, prepared to strike in force at any point. The first test came in May, when the Japanese made an attempt from the sea to take Port Moresby. This was successfully countered in the great carrier battle of the Coral Sea. Thereupon the Japanese struck eastward, hoping to destroy the U.S. Pacific Fleet and to seize Midway — a bid for naval supremacy in the Pacific. A diversionary attack on Dutch Harbor, the most forward U.S. base in Alaska, caused considerable damage, and the Japanese were able to occupy the islands of Kiska and Attu in the foggy Aleutian chain. But the main Japanese forces, far to the south, were crushingly defeated, with especially heavy losses in carriers and aircraft. The Battle of Midway in June 1942 was one of the truly decisive engagements of the war. By seriously weakening Japan's mobile striking forces, Midway left the Japanese virtually helpless to prevent the consolidation of American positions and the eventual development of overwhelming military supremacy throughout the Pacific. Only two months later, in fact, American forces took the first step on the long "road back" by landing on Guadalcanal in the southern Solomons.

Although the RAINBOW 5 plan was put into effect immediately after Pearl Harbor, the desperate situation in the Pacific and Far East and the shortage of shipping and escorts ruled out most of the scheduled Atlantic, Caribbean, and South American deployments. In January reinforcements were sent to Iceland and a token force to Northern Ireland, and by June two full divisions (the 34th Infantry and the 1st Armored) had reached Ireland, while the remainder of the 5th Infantry had arrived in Iceland, completing the relief of the U.S. Marine brigade and most of the British garrison. No more divisions sailed eastward until August. Meanwhile, garrisons in the Atlantic and Caribbean were being built up to war strength. But plans to occupy the Azores, Canaries, and Cape Verdes, and to capture Dakar on the west African coast went by the board, primarily for lack of shipping. Also abandoned after lengthy discussion was a project (GYMNAST) proposed by Prime Minister Churchill at the ARCADIA Conference for an Anglo-American occupation of French North Africa.

Thus, despite the reaffirmation of the "Germany first" strategy at ARCADIA, the great bulk of American forces sent overseas during the first half of 1942 went to the theaters of war against Japan. Of the eight Army divisions that left the country before August, five went to the Pacific. Including two more already in Hawaii, and a Marine division at sea, bound for New Zealand (eventually for the landings on Guadalcanal in August), eight divisions were deployed against Japan in July 1942. Of the approximately 520,000 Army troops in overseas bases, 60 percent were in the Pacific (including Alaska) and the newly established China-Burma-India theater; the remainder were almost all in Caribbean and western Atlantic garrisons. Of 2,200 Army aircraft overseas, about 1,300 were in the Pacific (including Alaska) and Far East, 900 in the western Atlantic and Latin America. Not until August did the U.S. Army Air Forces in the British Isles attain sufficient strength to fly a single independent bombing mission over northern France.

Planning for a Cross-Channel Invasion

The Army's leaders and planners, schooled in a tradition that emphasized the principles of mass and offensive, had been fretting over the scale of deployment to the Pacific since early in the year. Late in January Brig. Gen. Dwight D. Eisenhower, then a War Department staff officer whom General Marshall had assigned to handle the crisis in the Pacific, noted, "We've got to go to Europe and fight — and we've got to quit wasting resources all over the world." In the joint committees Army planners urged that as soon as the situation could be stabilized in the Southwest Pacific, U.S. forces should begin to concentrate in the British Isles for an offensive against Germany. Secretary Stimson and others were pressing the same views on the President. In the middle of March the Joint Chiefs of Staff approved this course of action, and in April, at the President's order, General Marshall and Harry Hopkins, the President's personal representative, went to London to seek British approval.

Logistical considerations heavily favored both the general strategy of concentration against Germany and the specific plan of invading northwestern Europe from a base in the British Isles. Because the target area was close to the main sources of British and American power, two to three times as many forces could be hurled against northwestern Europe, with a given amount of shipping, as could be supported in operations against Japan. Britain itself was a highly industrialized country, fully mobilized after two and a half years of war, and well shielded by air and naval power — a ready-made base for a land invasion and air attacks on Germany's vitals. While invasion forces were assembling, moreover, they would serve to garrison the British Isles. Finally, an attack across the English Channel would use the only short water crossing to the Continent from a base already available and would thrust directly at the heart of Fortress Europe by the main historic invasion routes.

Even so, the plan was a desperate gamble. If northwestern

Europe offered the Allies a position of strength, the Germans, too, would be strong there, close to their own heartland, served by the superb rail and road net of western and central Europe, shielded by submarines based along the entire length of Europe's Atlantic front. The limited range of fighter aircraft based in southern England narrowly restricted the choice of landing areas. Much hinged on the USSR, where for the present the bulk of Germany's land forces were pinned down. If the Soviet Union collapsed, an invasion from the west would be a suicidal venture. The invasion must therefore be launched before the Soviet armies were crushed and, moreover, in sufficient strength to draw substantial German forces away from the Eastern Front in order to avert that very catastrophe.

On the face of it, these two requirements seemed to cancel each other. For Allied planners had little hope that the Russians could stand up under another summer's onslaught, and it was obvious, in view of the scarcity of shipping, that any attack the Western Allies could mount by the coming summer or early fall would be hardly more than a pinprick. The best solution General Marshall's planners could offer to this dilemma was to set the invasion for the spring of 1943 (ROUNDUP), in the hope that until then, through air bombardment of Germany and a continued flow of matériel to the Soviet Union, the Allies could help the Soviet armies to stave off defeat. If these measures should fail, and Soviet resistance seemed about to collapse, then, with whatever forces were on hand, the Allies would have to invade the Continent in 1942 (SLEDGEHAMMER) — and no later than September, before bad weather closed down over the Channel. The same course would be followed in the unlikely event that Germany itself showed signs of serious weakness in 1942.

In London, Mr. Hopkins and General Marshall found the British delighted that the United States was ready to commit itself to a major offensive against Germany in 1943. The British readily agreed that preparations should begin immediately for an invasion the following spring, and they undertook to provide more than half the shipping needed to move about a million American troops and immense quantities of matériel to the United Kingdom. They warned, however, that their first concern at present was to maintain their position in the Middle East, where, late in January, Rommel's revitalized Africa Korps had inflicted a serious reverse on the

Eighth Army. Both sides were now feverishly building up for a new offensive. The British also expressed deep misgivings over the proposed emergency cross-Channel operation in the fall. Nevertheless, the British approved the American plan, essentially the War Department's plan, "in principle" — a phrase that was to give much trouble in the coalition war. The immediate relief felt by General Marshall's staff in Washington was reflected by General Eisenhower, then Chief, Operations Division, War Department General Staff, who noted: ". . . at long last, and after months of struggle . . . we are all definitely committed to one concept of fighting! If we can agree on major purposes and objectives, our efforts will begin to fall in line and we won't just be thrashing around in the dark."

But on the American side, too, there were strong reservations. Admiral King did not contest in principle the "Germany first" strategy. But he was determined not to allow preparations for the cross-Channel invasion to jeopardize "vital needs" in the Pacific, by which, as he candidly stated early in May, he meant the ability of U.S. forces "to hold what we have against any attack that the Japanese are capable of launching." Only the President's peremptory order on May 6 that the invasion build-up in Britain must not be slowed down (it had, indeed, scarcely begun) prevented a large-scale diversion of forces and shipping to the Pacific to counter the Japanese offensive that culminated in the great naval battles of the Coral Sea and Midway. The President himself made it clear, on the other hand, that aid to the Soviet Union would have to continue on a mounting scale, whatever the cost to BOLERO (the American build-up in the United Kingdom) in matériel and shipping. And even Army leaders were unwilling to assign shipping for the movement until the scheduled build-up of garrisons in the Western Hemisphere and various other overseas stations had been completed, which, it was estimated, would not be until August at the earliest. Until then British shipping would have to carry the main burden.

Not until June 1942, therefore, did the first shipload of American troops under the new plan set sail for England in the great British luxury liner, *Queen Elizabeth*. Almost simultaneously a new crisis erupted in the Middle East. At the end of May, after a four-month lull, Rommel seized the initiative and swept around the southern flank of the British Eighth Army, which held strong positions in eastern Libya from El Gazala on the coast south to Bir Hacheim. After two weeks of hard fighting, in which the British seemed to be holding their own, Rommel succeeded in taking Bir Hacheim, the southern anchor of the British line. During the next few days British armor, committed piecemeal in an effort to cover a withdrawal to the northeast, was virtually wiped out by skillfully concealed German 88-mm. guns. The Eighth Army once again retreated across the Egyptian frontier, and on June 21 Tobruk, which the British had expected, as in 1941, to hold out behind Axis lines, was captured with its garrison and large stores of trucks, gasoline, and other supplies.

News of this disaster reached Prime Minister Churchill in Washington, where he had gone early in the month to tell the President that the British were unwilling to go through with an emergency cross-Channel landing late in 1942. General Marshall immediately offered to send an armored division to help the hard-pressed British in Egypt, but it was decided, for the present, to limit American aid to emergency shipments of tanks, artillery, and the ground components of three combat air groups. This move required the diversion for many weeks of a substantial amount of U.K. shipping from the North Atlantic on the long voyage around the Cape of Good Hope. But the heaviest impact on the invasion build-up in the United Kingdom resulted from the diversion of British shipping to the Middle East and the retention there of shipping the British had earmarked for the build-up. For the time being, British participation in the BOLERO program virtually ceased.

By the end of August, with only seven months to go before the invasion was to be launched, only about 170,000 American troops were in or on their way to the British Isles, and the shipment of equipment and supplies, particularly for the development of cantonments, airfields, and base facilities, was hopelessly behind schedule. There seemed little likelihood that enough shipping would be available to complete the movement across the Atlantic of a million troops, with the ten to fifteen million tons of cargo that must accompany them, by April 1943 as scheduled. And even if the shipping could have been found, Britain's ports and inland transportation system would have been swamped before the influx reached its peak. Thus, by the late summer of 1942, a spring 1943 ROUNDUP appeared to be a logistical impossibility.

Torch Replaces Sledgehammer-Roundup

By this time, in fact, American military leaders had become discouraged about a cross-Channel invasion in spring of 1943, though not primarily because of the lag in the build-up program. In June the British had decided that SLEDGEHAMMER, for which they had never had any enthusiasm, could not be undertaken except in a situation which offered good prospects of success — that is, if the Germans should seem about to collapse. At the moment, with the German summer offensive just starting to roll toward the Caucasus and the lower Don, such a situation did not appear to be an imminent possibility. The British decision was influenced in part by the alarming lag in deliveries of American landing craft, of which less than two-thirds of the promised quota for the operation was expected to materialize. The British also argued that the confusion and losses attendant upon executing SLEDGEHAMMER — and the cost of supporting the beachhead once it was established — were likely to disrupt preparations for the main invasion the following spring. Since SLEDGEHAMMER, if carried out, would have to be, in the main, a British undertaking, the British veto was decisive. The operation was canceled.

As a substitute, the British proposed a less risky venture — landings in French North Africa — which they were confident could be accomplished in stride, without harm to ROUNDUP. To Stimson, Marshall, King, and Arnold this proposal was anathema. Failure would be a costly, perhaps fatal rebuff to Allied prestige. Success might be even more dangerous, the Americans feared, for it might lead the Allies step by step into a protracted series of operations around the southern periphery of Europe, operations that could not be decisive and would only postpone the final test of strength with Germany. At the very least, an invasion of North Africa would, the Americans were convinced, rule out a spring 1943 invasion of the Continent. The Army planners preferred the safer alternative of simply reinforcing the British in Egypt.

The British proposal was, nevertheless, politically shrewd, for it was no secret that President Roosevelt had long ago expressed a predilection for this very undertaking. He was determined, besides, that American ground forces go into action somewhere in the European area before the end of 1942. Already half persuaded, he hardly needed Churchill's enthusiastic rhetoric to win him over to the new project. When General Marshall and his colleagues in the Joint Chiefs of Staff suggested, as an alternative, that the United States should immediately go on the defensive in Europe and turn all-out against Japan, Roosevelt brusquely rejected the idea.

In mid-July, Hopkins, Marshall, and King went to London under orders from the President to reach agreement with the British on some operation in 1942. After a vain effort to persuade the British to reconsider an invasion of the Continent in 1942, the Americans reluctantly agreed on July 24 to the North Africa operation, now christened TORCH, to be launched before the end of October. The President, overruling Marshall's suggestion that final decision be postponed until mid-September in order to permit a reappraisal of the Soviet situation, cabled Hopkins that he was "delighted" and that the orders were now "full speed ahead." Into the final agreement, however, Marshall and King wrote their own conviction that the decision on TORCH "in all probability" ruled out invasion of the Continent in 1943 and meant, further, that the Allies had accepted "a defensive, encircling line of action" in the European-Mediterranean war.

End of the Defensive Stage

With the decision for TORCH, the first stage in the search for a strategic plan against Germany came to an end. In retrospect, 1941-42 had been a period of defensive strategy, and a strategy of scarcity. The British and American approaches to war had had their first conflict, and the British had won the first round. That British notions of strategy had tended to prevail was not surprising. British forces had been mobilized earlier and were in the theaters in far greater numbers than American forces. The United States was still mobilizing its manpower and resources. It had taken the better part of the year after Pearl Harbor for U.S. forces to have an appreciable effect in the theaters. Strategic planning in 1942 had been largely opportunistic, hand to mouth, and limited by critical shortages in shipping and munitions. Troops had been parceled out piecemeal to meet immediate threats and crises. Despite the "Germany first" decision, the total U.S. Army forces deployed in the war against Japan by the end of the year actually exceeded the total U.S. Army forces deployed in the war against Germany. The one scheme to put Allied planning on an orderly, long-range basis and to achieve the concepts of mass and concentration in which General Marshall and his staff had put their faith had failed. By the close of the critical first year after Pearl Harbor, an effective formula for halting the dissipation of forces and matériel in what it regarded as secondary ventures still eluded the Army high command.

CHAPTER 3

Grand Strategy and the Washington High Command

In 1943 the debate within the Grand Alliance over strategy against the Axis Powers entered a new stage. The midwar period — roughly to the establishment of a foothold in Normandy in the summer of 1944 — was the period of increasing plenty. The power to call the turn on strategy and to choose the time and place to do battle passed to the Allies. U.S. troops and supplies flowed out in ever-increasing numbers and quantity, and the full impact of American mobilization and production was felt not only in the theaters but also in Allied councils. But the transition to the strategic initiative introduced many new and complex problems for the high command in Washington. Active and passive fronts were now established all over the world. The TORCH decision had thrown all Allied planning into a state of uncertainty. For General Marshall and the Army planners in the Washington command post the basic strategic question was how to limit operations in subsidiary theaters and carry the war decisively to the Axis Powers. They had to start over and seek new and firmer long-range bases upon which to plan for victory in the multifront coalition war.

The decision for TORCH opened a great debate on European strategy between the Americans and the British that endured down to the summer of 1944. The issues that emerged were disputed in and out of the big international conferences of midwar from Casablanca in January 1943 to Second Quebec in September 1944. In that debate Churchill eloquently urged ever onward in the Mediterranean — Sicily, landing in Italy, Rome, the Pisa-Rimini line; then "north and northeast." President Roosevelt, himself fascinated by the possibilities in the Mediterranean, to a considerable extent seconded these moves, despite the reluctance of the American Chiefs. Pleading his case skillfully, the British leader stressed the need to continue the momentum, the immediate advantages, the "great prizes" to be picked up in the Mediterranean, the need to continue the softening-up process, while the Allies awaited a favorable opportunity to invade the Continent across the English Channel. The fact that sizable Allied forces were present in the Mediterranean and that there was an immediate chance to weaken the enemy in that area were telling arguments.

At the same time the Americans — with General Marshall as the foremost military spokesman — gradually made progress toward limiting the Mediterranean advance, toward directing it to the west rather than to the east, toward linking it directly with a definite major cross-Channel operation, and thereby winning their way back to the idea of waging a war of mass and concentration on the Continent. Part of their task was to secure agreement with President Roosevelt, part with the British, and eventually the Russians. The series of decisions reached at the 1943 conferences — Casablanca in January, Washington (TRIDENT) in May, First Quebec (QUADRANT) in August, and Cairo-Tehran (SEXTANT-EUREKA) in November and December — reflect the compromises of the Americans and the British between opportunism and long-range commitments, between a war of attrition and a war of mass and concentration.

Each of these conferences marked a milestone in coalition strategy and in the maturation of American strategic planning. At Casablanca General Marshall made a last vigorous but vain stand for a cross-Channel operation in 1943. The conferees did approve a round-the-clock combined bomber offensive against Germany that both the Americans and the British viewed as a prerequisite to a future cross-Channel operation. But no real long-range plan for the defeat of the Axis Powers emerged. Casablanca merely recognized that the Anglo-Americans would retain the initiative in the Mediterranean, and defined the short-range objective in terms of a prospective operation against Sicily.

Unlike the small, disunited American delegation, the well-prepared British operated as a cohesive team and presented a united front. President Roosevelt, still attracted to the Mediterranean, had not yet made the notion of a big cross-Channel attack his own. A striking illustration of the want of understanding between the White House and the military staffs came in connection with the unconditional surrender formula to which he and Churchill publicly committed themselves at Casablanca. The President had simply informed the JCS of his intention to support that concept as the basic Allied aim in the war at a meeting at the White House shortly before the conference. But no study of the meaning of this formula for the conduct of the war was made by either the Army or the Joint Staff before or during the conference — nor did the President encourage his military advisers to do so.

To the American military staff it appeared at the time that the long experience of the British in international negotiations had carried the day. Keenly disappointed, Brig. Gen. Albert C. Wedemeyer, General Marshall's principal adviser at Casablanca, wrote: ". . . we lost our shirts and . . . are now committed to a subterranean umbilicus operation in midsummer. . . . we came, we listened, and we were conquered."

General Wedemeyer admired the way the British had presented their case: "They swarmed down upon us like locusts with a plentiful supply of planners and various other assistants with prepared plans. . . . As an American I wish that we might be more glib and better organized to cope with these super negotiators. From a worm's eye viewpoint it was apparent that we were confronted by generations and generations of experience in committee work and in rationalizing points of view. They had us on the defensive practically all the time."

The American military staff took the lessons of Casablanca to heart. If they did not become more glib, they at least organized themselves better. To meet the British on more equal terms, they overhauled their joint planning system and resolved to reach closer understandings with the President in advance of future meetings. As a by-product of the debate and negotiation over grand strategy in midwar, the planning techniques and methods of the Americans became more nearly like those of their British ally, even if their strategic ideas still differed. They became more skilled in the art of military diplomacy, of quid pro quo, or what might be termed the "tactics" of strategic planning. At the same time their strategic thinking became more sophisticated. The Casablanca Conference represented the last fling for the "either-or" school of thought in the American military staff. Henceforth, they began to think not in terms of this *or* that operation, but in terms of this *and* that — or what one planner fittingly called "permutations and combinations." The outstanding strategic questions for them were no longer to be phrased in terms of either a Mediterranean or a cross-Channel operation, but in terms of defining the precise relations between them — and the Combined Bomber Offensive.

In the debate, the American Joint Chiefs of Staff countered British demands for more emphasis upon the Mediterranean, particularly the eastern Mediterranean, by supporting further development of Pacific offensives. Holding open the "Pacific alternative" carried with it the threat of non cross-Channel operation at all — which the British did not wish. The war in the Pacific thereby offered the United States staff a significant lever for keeping the Mediterranean issue under control. At the same time General Marshall recognized that the Mediterranean offensive could not be stopped completely with North Africa or Sicily and that definite advantages would accrue from knocking out Italy, opening up the Mediterranean further for Allied shipping, and widening the air offensive against Germany.

Beginning with the compromise agreements at TRIDENT in the spring of 1943, the American representatives could point to definite steps toward fixing European strategy in terms of a major cross-Channel undertaking for 1944. At that conference they assented to a plan for eliminating Italy from the war, which the British urged as the "great prize" after Sicily. But the forces, the Americans insisted, were to be limited so far as possible to those already in the Mediterranean. At the same time, they won British agreement to the transfer of 4 American and 3 British divisions from the Mediterranean to the United Kingdom. Both sides agreed to continue the Combined Bomber Offensive from the United Kingdom in four phases to be completed by April 1944 and leading up to an invasion across the Channel. Most encouraging was the President's unequivocal announcement in favor of a cross-Channel undertaking for the spring of 1944. The British agreed that planning should start for mounting such an operation with target date, May 1944, on the basis of 29 divisions built up in the United Kingdom (Operation ROUNDHAMMER, later called OVERLORD). The bare outlines of a new pattern of European strategy began to take shape.

That pattern took clearer shape at QUADRANT. There the American Chiefs urged a firm commitment to OVERLORD, the plan developed by a British-American planning staff in London. The British agreed but refused to give it the "overriding priority" over all operations in the Mediterranean area that the Americans desired. Plans were to proceed for eliminating Italy from the war, establishing bases as far north as Rome, seizing Sardinia and Corsica, and landing in southern France. Forces for these operations would be limited to those allotted at TRIDENT. With a definite limitation on the Mediterranean offensive, authorization for a definite allocation of forces for the approved cross-Channel operation, and for an extended Combined Bomber Offensive in support of it, the strategic pattern against Germany was taking on more final form.

After QUADRANT came new danger signals for the Washington high command. The British were making overtures for active operations in the Aegean, which the Americans interpreted, wrongly or rightly, as a prelude to a move on the Balkans and a consequent threat to the cross-Channel strategy. At the Moscow Conference in October 1943 came other warning signs from another and more unexpected source. At that meeting of the foreign ministers, a prelude to the full-dress conference at Tehran to follow, the representatives of the Anglo-American staffs met for the first time with the Russian staff. In a surprise maneuver, the Russians, who from the beginning had been pleading for the second front in Europe, intimated that they might be willing to accept an active campaign in Italy as the second front.

With these portents in mind, the uneasy American Joint Chiefs

TEHRAN CONFERENCES

of Staff accompanied the President on board the USS *Iowa* en route to the Cairo Conference in November 1943. During the rehearsals on that voyage for the meetings ahead the President afforded his military advisers a rare glimpse into his reflections on the political problems that were bound up with the war and its outcome. His concern lest the United States be drawn into a permanent or lengthy occupation of Europe came out sharply in the discussion with the JCS on the zones of occupation in postwar Germany. As he told the JCS, "We should not get roped into accepting any European sphere of influence." Nor did he wish the United States to become involved in a prolonged task of reconstituting France, Italy, and the Balkans. "France," he declared, "is a British baby." Significantly, the President added, "There would definitely be a race for Berlin. We may have to put the United States Divisions into Berlin as soon as possible." With a pencil he quickly sketched on a simple map of Europe the zonal boundaries he envisaged, putting Berlin and Leipzig in a big American zone in northern Germany — one of the most unusual records of the entire war and later brought back to Washington by Army officers in the American delegation.

56

Tehran proved to be the decisive conference in European strategy. There, for the first time in the war, President Roosevelt, Prime Minister Churchill, and their staffs met with Marshal Stalin, the Soviet leader, and his staff. Churchill made eloquent appeals for operations in Italy, the Aegean, and the east Mediterranean, even at the expense of a delay in OVERLORD. For reasons of its own, the USSR put its weight behind the American concept of strategy. Confident of its capabilities, demonstrated in its great comeback since the critical days of Stalingrad, the Soviet Union asserted its full power as an equal member of the Allied coalition. Stalin came out vigorously in favor of OVERLORD and limiting further operations in the Mediterranean to one directly assisting OVERLORD, an invasion of southern France. In turn, the Russians promised to launch an all-out offensive on their front to accompany the Allied moves. Stalin's strong stand put the capstone on Western strategy against Germany. The Anglo-American Chiefs agreed to launch OVERLORD during May 1944 in conjunction with a southern France operation, and to consider these the supreme operations for that year.

The final blueprint for Allied victory in Europe had taken shape. Germany was to be crushed between the jaws of a gigantic vise applied from the west and the east. How much reliance President Roosevelt had come to place in General Marshall was reflected in his decision not to release Marshall for the command of the cross-Channel attack. As he told General Marshall, "I . . . could not sleep at night with you out of the country." President Roosevelt gave the nod to General Eisenhower, who had built a solid reputation as the successful leader of coalition forces in the Mediterranean. Preparations for the big cross-Channel attack began in earnest.

The last lingering issue in the long drawn-out debate was not settled until the summer of 1944. In the months following Tehran, the southern France operation came perilously close to being abandoned in favor of the British desire for further exploitation in Italy and possibly even across the Julian Alps into the Hungarian plain. Complicating the picture was a shortage of landing craft to carry of both OVERLOAD and the southern France attack simultaneously. But General Marshall and the Washington military authorities, backed by President Roosevelt, remained adamant on the southern attack. The British and the Americans did not reach final agreement on a outhernFrance operation until August — two months after the OVERLORD landings — just a few days before the operation was actually launched, when Churchill reluctantly yielded. This concluding phase of the debate represented the last gasp of the peripheral strategy with a new and sharper political twist. Churchill was now warily watching the changing European scene with one eye on the retreating Germans, and the other on the advancing Russians.

A number of misconceptions grew up in the postwar period about this Anglo-American debate over strategy. What was at stake in the midwar debate was not whether there should be a cross-Channel operation. Rather the question was: Should that operation be a full-bodied drive with a definite target date that the Americans desired, or a final blow to an enemy critically weakened in a war of opportunity that the British desired? It is a mistake to assume that the British did not from the first want a cross-Channel operation. The difference lay essentially in the precise timing of that attack and in the extent and direction of preparatory operations. Once agreed on the major blow, the British stoutly held out for a strong initial assault that would insure success in the operation. It is also a mistake to assume that the Americans remained opposed to all Mediterranean operations. Indeed, much of their effort in 1943-44 was spent in reconciling those operations with a prospective cross-Channel operation.

What about the question of a Balkan alternative that has aroused so much controversy? Would it not have been wiser to have invaded the continent through the Balkans and thereby forestall Soviet domination? The fact must be emphasized that this is a postwar debate. The Balkan invasion was never proposed by any responsible leader in Allied strategy councils as an alternative to OVERLORD; nor did any Allied debate or combined planning take place in those terms. After the war Churchill steadfastly denied that he wanted a Balkan invasion. The British contended that the Americans had been frightened by the specter rather than by the substance of their proposals. And indeed the American staff had been frightened by the implications of Churchillian proposals for raids, assistance to native populations, throwing in a few armored divisions, and the like — for the eastern Mediterranean and Balkan regions. For the American staff Mediterranean operations had offered a striking demonstration of how great the costs of a war of attrition could be. The so-called "soft underbelly" of Italy, to which the Prime Minister had glowingly referred, turned out to be a hard-shelled back demanding more and more increments of American and Allied men and means. The mere thought of being sucked step by step, by design or by circumstance, into a similar undertaking in the Balkans, an area of poor terrain and communications — even if it were an unrealistic fear on the part of the American staff — was enough to send shivers up the spines of American planners. Certainly, neither the President nor the American staff wanted to get involved in the thorny politics of the Balkan area, and both were determined to stay out. The Balkan question was never argued out in frank military or political terms by the Allies during World War II.

Frustrated by the loss of what he regarded as glittering opportunities in the Mediterranean, Churchill struck out after the war at the American wartime "logical, large-scale mass-production thinking." But as Gordon Harrison, the author of *Cross-Channel Attack,* put it: "To accuse Americans of mass-production thinking is only to accuse them of having a mass-production economy and of recognizing the military advantage of such an economy. The Americans were power-minded." From the beginning they thought in terms of taking on the main German armies and beating them. Back of the American staff's fear of a policy of attritional and peripheral warfare against Germany in midwar lay their continued anxiety over its ultimate costs in men, resources, and time. This anxiety was increased by their concern with getting on with the war against Japan. Basic in their thinking was a growing realization of the ultimate limits of American manpower and a growing anxiety about the effects of a long-continued period of maximum mobilization on the home front. All of these factors combined to confirm their faith in the doctrine of military concentration.

As it turned out, the final strategy against Germany was a compromise of American and British views — of British peripheral strategy and the American principle of concentration. To the extent that the cross-Channel operation was delayed a year later than the Americans wished in order to take advantage of Mediterranean opportunities and to continue the softening up process, the British prevailed. Perhaps still haunted by the ghosts of Passchendaele and

59

Dunkerque, the British were particularly sensitive to the requisite conditions for OVERLORD — for example, how many enemy troops could be expected to oppose it. But, as the Americans had hoped from the beginning, the cross-Channel attack turned out to be a conclusive operation with a fixed target date; it was given the highest priority and the maximum force to drive directly at the heart of German power.

Thus, by the summer of 1944 the final blueprinting of the Allied strategy for defeating Germany was completed. Despite the compromises with opportunism, American staff notions of fighting a concentrated, decisive war had been clearly written into the final pattern. Those notions had been reinforced by the addition, from Casablanca onward, of the unconditional surrender aim. The peripheral trend had been brought under control, and General Marshall had managed to conserve American military power for the big cross-Channel blow. The Americans had learned to deal with the British on more nearly equal terms. The military chiefs had drawn closer to the President and the U.S. side was able to present a united front vis-a-vis the British.

During the Anglo-American debate of midwar, significant changes had taken place in the alignment of power within the Grand Alliance. These shifts had implications as important for war strategy as for future relations among the wartime partners. By the close of 1943 the mighty American industrial and military machine was in high gear. The growing flow of American military strength and supplies to the European theater assured the acceptance of the American strategic concept. The Soviet Union, steadily gathering strength and confidence in 1943, made its weight felt at a critical point in the strategic debate. Britain had virtually completed its mobilization by the end of 1943, and stresses and strains had begun to appear in its economy. Compared to the Soviet Union and the United States, Britain was becoming relatively weaker. In midwar the Americans drew up with and threatened to pass the British in deployed strength in the European theater. Within the coalition Britain's military power and notions of fighting the war were being overtaken. Tehran, which fixed the final European strategy, marked a subtle but important change in the foundations of the Alliance. For the strategists of the Pentagon and of the Kremlin the doctrine of concentration had provided a common bond.

Completing the Strategic Patterns

From the standpoint of the Washington high command, the main story of military strategy in World War II, except for the important and still unanswered question of how to defeat Japan, came to an end in the summer of 1944. The last stage — culminating in the surrender of Germany and of Japan — was the period of the payoff, of the unfolding of strategy in the field. In this final phase, the problems of winning the war began to run up against the problems of winning the peace.

Once the Allied forces became firmly lodged on the European continent and took up the pursuit of the German forces, the war became for General Marshall and his staff essentially a matter of tactics and logistics — the Supreme Allied Commander, General Eisenhower, assuming the responsibility for making decisions as military circumstances in the field dictated. But to Churchill, disturbed by the swift Soviet advance into Poland and the Balkans, the war seemed more than ever a contest for great political stakes. In the last year of the European conflict therefore, the two approaches often became a question of military tactics versus political considerations.

By the summer of 1944 the shape of things to come was already apparent. Once on the Continent, General Eisenhower was given more and more responsibility for political decisions, or fell heir to them by default. Lacking political guidance and direction from Washington, the commander in the field made decisions on the basis of military considerations. He fell back on the U.S. staff notions of defeating the enemy and ending the war quickly and decisively with the fewest casualties. This trend became even more marked in 1945 in the commander's decision to stop at the Elbe and not attempt to take Berlin or Prague ahead of the Russians.

As usual, General Marshall and the U.S. staff backed the decisions of the commander in the field. Typical of Marshall's approach were two statements he made in April 1945 — one in response to a British proposal to capture Berlin, the other concerning the liberation of Prague. With reference to Berlin, Marshall joined with his colleagues in the JCS in emphasizing to the British Chiefs of Staff "that the destruction of the German armed forces is more important than any political or psychological advantages which might be derived from possible capture of the German capital ahead of the Russians. . . . Only Eisenhower is in a position to make a decision concerning his battle and the best way to exploit successes to the full." With respect to Prague, Marshall wrote to Eisenhower "Personally and aside from all logistic, tactical or strategic implications, I would be loath to hazard American lives for purely political purposes." Such views of the Army Chief of Staff took on added significance, for during Roosevelt's final and his successor's early days in office the burden of dealing with important issues fell heavily on the senior military advisers in the Washington high command. Marshall's stand on these issues was entirely consistent with earlier Army strategic planning. Whatever the ultimate political outcome, from the standpoint of a decisive military conclusion of the war against Germany it made little difference whether the forces of the United States or those of the Soviet Union took Berlin and Prague. At the same time, in purely military dealings with the Russians in the closing months of the European conflict, and as Soviet and American troops drew closer, the American staff began to stiffen its stand and a firmer note crept into its negotiations for coordination of Allied efforts. Early in 1945 Marshall advised Eisenhower to forget diplomatic niceties in dealing with the Russians and urged him to adopt a direct approach "in simple Main Street Abilene style."

Churchill's inability to reverse the course of the last year of the war underscored the changed relationships between U.S. and British national military weight and the shifting bases of the Grand Alliance. With British manpower already mobilized to the hilt, after the middle of 1944 British production became increasingly unbalanced, and the British fought the remainder of the war with a contracting economy. The Americans did not hit the peak of their military manpower mobilization until May 1945 — the month Germany surrendered. Reaching their war production peak at the end of 1943, they were able to sustain it at high levels to the end of the war. The greater capacity of the American economy and population to support a sustained, large-scale Allied offensive effort showed up clearly in the last year of the European war. Once entrenched on the Continent, American divisions began to outnumber the British more and more. Through the huge stockpiles of

American production already built up and through his control of the growing U.S. military manpower on the Continent, General Eisenhower was able to put the imprint of U.S. staff thinking on how to win the war. Whatever his political predilections, Churchill had to yield. As the war against Germany lengthened beyond the hoped-for end in 1944, British influence in high Allied councils went into further decline. The last year of the war saw the United States and the Soviet Union emerging as the two strongest military powers in Europe, the one as intent on leaving Europe soon as the other was on pushing its strategic frontiers westward. On the Western side the struggle was to be concluded the way the American military chiefs had wished to wage it from the beginning — as a conventional war of concentration.

Meanwhile, as the war with Germany was drawing to a close, the strategy for defeating Japan had gradually been taking shape. Despite the Germany-first principle, the so-called secondary war simply would not stand still. From the beginning, in the defensive as well as in the offensive stage, the Pacific exerted a strong pull on American forces and resources. Nor would American public opinion tolerate a strictly defensive, limited war against Japan until Germany was beaten. Though final plans had to await the defeat of Germany, the pace of advance in the Pacific became so fast that it almost caught up with the European conflict. In the Pacific, as in the Mediterranean, American strategists learned that forces in being had a way of creating their own strategy.

While European war strategy was fashioned on the international level, the war against Japan from the beginning was almost exclusively an American affair, and its strategy essentially an interservice concern. The American plans and decisions in the Pacific war were presented to the international conferences, where they usually received Allied approval with little debate. Disputes and arguments were on the service level for the most part, with General Marshall and Admiral King working out compromises between themselves. In the process General Marshall often acted as mediator between the Navy and General MacArthur.

The traditional naval concern with the Pacific and the necessarily heavy reliance in the theater upon shipping, especially assault shipping, put the main burden of developing offensive strategy upon the Navy. But Navy plans for a central Pacific offensive had to be

MEDIUM TANKS ON AN AMERICAN ASSEMBLY LINE

reconciled with General MacArthur's concept of approaching Japan via the New Guinea-Philippines axis. Thus a twofold approach — "a one-two punch" — replaced the original single axis strategy. This double axis advance produced a strategy of opportunity similar to that urged by the British for the war in Europe and took the Allies to the threshold of Japan by the time the European war ended. The critical question of whether Japan could be defeated by bombardment and blockade alone, or whether an invasion would be necessary, was long debated. In Washington during the late spring of 1945 the Army's argument that plans and preparations should be made for an invasion was accepted as the safe course to follow.

64

The rapid pace of the Pacific advance outran the American plans for the China-Burma-India Theater, and that theater declined in strategic importance in the war against Japan. Disillusioned by the inability of China to play an active role in the final defeat of Japan, American military leaders sought to substitute the USSR. To save American lives in a Pacific OVERLORD, those leaders in general became eager to have the USSR enter the war against Japan and pin down Japanese forces on the Asiatic mainland. Before final plans for a Pacific OVERLORD could be put into effect, however, the Japanese surrendered. The dramatic dropping of atomic bombs on August 6 and 9 on Hiroshima and Nagasaki, respectively, came as a complete surprise to the American public and to the Army strategic planners, with the exception of a handful of top officers in the Washington command post who were in on the secret. In a sense the supersession of strategic plans by a revolutionary development of weapons was a fitting climax to a war that had throughout shown a strong tendency to go its own way.

The last year of the war witnessed, along with the finishing touches on grand strategy, the change-over from the predominantly military to the politico-military phase. As victory loomed, stresses and strains within the coalition became more apparent. With the Second Quebec Conference in September 1944 agreement among the Allies on military plans and war strategy became less urgent than need to arrive at acceptable politico-military terms on which the winning powers could continue to collaborate. That need became even more marked at Yalta in February 1945 and at the Potsdam Conference in July 1945. To handle these new challenges after building up a staff mechanism geared to the predominantly military business of fighting a global and coalition war necessitated considerable adjustment of Army staff processes and planning. In midwar Army planning had been geared to achieve the decisive blow on the Continent that had been a cardinal element in the planners' strategic faith. Scarcely were the Western Allies ensconced on the Continent, however, when the challenges of victory and peace were upon the Army planners. They entered the last year of the war with the coalition disintegrating, the President failing in health, and a well-organized politico-military machine lacking. Besides the frictions generating on the foreign fronts, the Army still had to cope with the immense problem of what to do with the beaten foe — with terms of surrender, occupation, and postwar bases. The military fell heir — by default — to problems no longer easily divided into military and political.

Expansion and Distribution of the Wartime Army

To the Washington high command strategic plans were one vital ingredient in the formula for victory. Manpower was another. Indeed, at stake in the midwar debate was the fresh and flexible military power of the United States. That power was also General Marshall's trump card in negotiations with the coalition partners. To put a brake on diversionary deployments to secondary theaters and ventures and to conserve American military manpower for the big cross-Channel blow became the major preoccupation of the Chief of Staff and his advisers in midwar. Behind their concern for effective presentation of the American strategic case at the midwar international conferences lay the growing uneasiness of General Marshall and his staff over the American manpower problem. To continue what appeared to them to be essentially a policy of drift in Allied strategy raised grave issues about mobilizing and deploying U.S. forces. To support a war of attrition and peripheral action, in place of concentrated effort, raised serious problems about the size and kind of Army the United States should and could maintain.

To establish a proper manpower balance for the United States in wartime was as difficult as it was important. In light of the 15 to 16 million men estimated to be physically fit for active military service, on the surface it seemed hard to understand why there should be any U.S. manpower problem at all. The problem as well as the answer stemmed basically from the fact that the Allies had from the beginning accepted the proposition that the single greatest tangible asset the United States brought to the coalition in World War II was the productive capacity of its industry. From the very beginning, U.S. manpower calculations had to be closely correlated with the needs of war industry.

The Army had therefore to compete for manpower not only with the needs of the other services but also with the claims of industry. By 1943 the "arsenal of democracy" was just beginning to hit its full productive stride. To cut too deeply into the industrial manpower of the country in order to furnish men for the Army and Navy might interfere seriously with arming U.S. and Allied troops. Furthermore, the United States was fighting a global conflict. To service its lines of communications extending around the world required large numbers of men, and great numbers of troops were constantly in transit to and from the theaters. To carry the fight across the oceans demanded a powerful Navy and a large merchant fleet, which also had to be given a high priority for manpower. Each industry as well as each theater commander was continually calling for more men. The problem for the Army was not only how much it should receive for its share of the manpower pool but also how it should divide that share most effectively to meet the diverse demands made upon it.

By 1943 the realization among the Army staff was growing that the U.S. manpower barrel did have a bottom. Even before the end of 1942 it was becoming visible. Also evident was the fact that, while the United States would remain the major "arsenal of democracy," it could no longer be regarded as a limitless source of munitions. The pool of unemployed that had cushioned the shock of mobilization for three years had been almost exhausted. Industrial expansion had slowed down, labor had become tight in many areas, and in November 1942 the President had placed a ceiling of 8.2 million officers and men upon the Army's expansion during 1943, intimating at the same time that this limit would probably hold for the duration of the war. General Marshall and his colleagues in the JCS were still determined that the United States make a major contribution in fighting forces to the defeat of the Axis Powers. But postponement of the invasion of northwestern Europe, together with the indicated limitations on American manpower and resources, made it necessary to reconsider the nature of that contribution. To match strategy, manpower, and production for the offensive phase of the war became a basic task of the Washington high command in the remainder of the war.

Supply programs for 1943 reflected prospective changes in the American role in the war. Cuts fell most heavily on the ground munitions program, which was reduced by more than one-fifth, and on lend-lease to nations other than the Soviet Union. Some reductions were also made in naval ship construction, but the program for building escort vessels was left intact and the merchant ship-building program was actually enlarged. The emphasis was on producing first of all the tools needed to defeat the U-boats and secure the sea lanes for the deployment of American forces overseas, and at the same time to insure that ample shipping would be available for this purpose. Soviet armies had to be assured a continuous flow of munitions to enable them to stave off the Germans. Meanwhile, airpower had to be built up and brought to bear as rapidly as possible, while the slower mobilization and deployment of ground forces was under way — heavy bombers to batter the German homeland, carrier-borne aircraft to restore mobility and striking power to the forces in the Pacific. The ground army, finally, had to be shaped to operate, at least during the coming year and a half, in relatively small packages at the end of long lines of communications in a great variety of terrain. Its units had to be compact, versatile, and easily transportable, but also mobile and able to hit hard. Every ton of shipping, as General McNair declared, had to deliver the maximum of fighting power.

The changing requirements and circumstances of coalition warfare in the offensive phase greatly affected plans and programs for expanding the U.S. Army — in total growth and internal distribution of strength as well as in overseas deployment. Manpower squeezes, together with strategic, logistical, and operational considerations, helped to change the shape as well as the size of the Army. By the end of 1942 the U.S. Army had grown to a strength of 5.4 million officers and men. Although this was still well under the ceiling of 8.2 million set by the President in November, the mobilization of ground combat elements was already nearing completion. Seventy-three divisions were then in being, and no more than 100 were expected to be activated. In June 1943 the goal was reduced to 90 divisions, with an overall strength ceiling of 7.7 million — far under the heavily mechanized force of 215 divisions which the framers of the Victory Program in 1941 had considered none too large to take on the German Army. Actually the U.S. Army in 1945 reached a peak strength of 8.3 million and 89 divisions. The last division was activated in August 1943.

The strength of ground combat units in the Army increased hardly at all after 1942, even though 16 divisions and some 350 separate artillery and engineer battalions were added after that date. These additional units had to be formed by means of redistribution and economies within existing personnel allotments in the

68

same categories. Since the Army as a whole increased by almost 3 million men after 1942, its ground combat elements, even including replacements, declined from over half of the Army's total strength at the beginning of 1942 to about a third in the spring of 1945. It was no mean achievement merely to maintain the Army's combat units at full strength during the heavy fighting of 1944 and 1945. Neither the Germans nor the Japanese were able to do as much.

Mindful of the untrained divisions sent overseas in World War I, General Marshall from the first set as his goal thorough and realistic training of large units in the United States, culminating in large-scale maneuvers by corps and armies. Since all divisions had been activated by August 1943 and the mass deployment of the Army overseas did not begin until late in that year, most divisions were thoroughly trained. The major threat to an orderly training program came in 1944 when many trained divisions had to be skeletonized in order to meet the demand for trained replacements. Equipment shortages were a serious obstacle to effective training in early 1943, as in 1942, as was also the shortage of trained commissioned and noncommissioned officers to provide cadres.

In 1943 the Army's ground combat forces continued to undergo the drastic reorganization and streamlining begun in 1942. Troop basis cuts reduced the planned number of armored divisions from 20 to 16, eliminated all motorized divisions, and cut back tank destroyer and antiaircraft units. The armored corps disappeared. Armored and infantry divisions were reduced in personnel and equipment. Tanks taken from armored divisions were organized into separate tank battalions, to be attached to divisions as needed, and motor transport was pooled under corps or army headquarters for greater flexibility.

The division remained the basic fighting team of arms and services combined in proportions designed for continuous offensive action under normal battle conditions. Its triangular organization was retained. The infantry division contained 3 regiments, and included, besides 4 artillery battalions (3 armed with 105-mm. howitzers, 1 with 155-mm. howitzers), a reconnaissance troop (scout cars and light tanks), and engineer, ordnance, signal, quartermaster, medical, and military police units. Each regiment could readily be teamed with an artillery battalion. Reinforced with other elements of the division, or with elements assigned by corps or army headquarters, it formed the regimental combat team. The total strength of the infantry division was reduced from its prewar strength of 15,245 to 14,253.

The armored division, as organized in 1942, had consisted of 2 tank regiments and 1 armored infantry regiment, plus 3 battalions of armored artillery and an armored reconnaissance battalion. This arrangement was calculated to produce 2 combat commands, with varying proportions of tanks and infantry in division reserve. The armored division also included supporting elements corresponding to those in the infantry divisions but motorized to increase mobility. In the armored division as reorganized in 1943, battalions replaced regiments. The new model contained 3 medium tank battalions, 3 armored infantry battalions, and 3 armored artillery battalions. These, with supporting elements, could be combined readily into 3 combat commands (A, B, and Reserve). The total strength of the armored division was reduced from 14,620 to 10,937. Two armored divisions remained "heavy" divisions, with the old organization, until the end of the war.

The only other special type of division of real importance retained in 1943 was the airborne division. Including parachute and gliderborne regiments, it was designed as a miniature infantry division, with lighter, more easily transportable artillery and the minimum of vehicles and service elements needed to keep it fighting after an airdrop until it could be reinforced. Its strength was only 8,500 until early 1945 when it was raised to 12,979. By the beginning of 1945 other experimental and special-type divisions — mountain, motorized, light, jungle, and cavalry — had either disappeared or largely lost their special characteristics.

Underlying all this change were the basic aims of making ground forces mobile, flexible, and easily transportable, by increasing the proportion of standardized and interchangeable units in less rigid tactical combinations. Nor did this streamlining involve any sacrifice of effective power. Army leaders were convinced, and experience on the whole proved, that these units could not only move faster and farther, but could also strike even harder than the units they replaced.

Premobilization planning had contemplated that Negro Americans would be included in the ranks of a wartime Army proportionately to their number in the whole population and proportionately, also, in each of the arms and services. Neither goal was achieved, but the number of Negro troops in the Army reached a peak strength of over 700,000 and more than 500,000 of them served overseas. Contemporary attitudes and practices in American society kept Negroes in segregated units throughout the war, although the Army gradually eliminated many of the obvious types of discrimination that almost inevitably flowed from their segregation. The bulk of Negro soldiers overseas were in supply and construction units; but many others who served in the two Negro divisions, in separate combat support battalions, and in a fighter group, directly engaged the enemy on the ground and in the air.

In 1944 the manpower shortage became nation-wide. The Army, under the double pressure of accelerated deployment schedules and heavy demands for infantry replacements for battle casualties in the two-front full-scale war, was driven to stringent measures. The Army Specialized Training Program, which had absorbed 150,000 soldiers in college study, was dissolved, and the aviation cadet training program was drastically curtailed. To release soldiers for battle, the Army drew heavily on limited service personnel and women for noncombat duties. The induction of female volunteers had begun in mid-1942 and in the following year, for the first time in the Army's history, women had been given a full legal military status as the Women's Army Corps (WAC). Growing in strength, the WAC reached a peak of 100,000 by the spring of 1945.

As the Army moved overseas, many posts were consolidated or closed, releasing large numbers of overhead personnel. Margins of overstrength and basic privates in tactical units were eliminated or reduced. Coast artillery units were converted to heavy artillery, hundreds of antiaircraft units were dissolved, and nondivisional infantry regiments became a source of infantry replacements. To meet the threat of the German counteroffensive in the Ardennes in December 1944, the handful of divisions remaining in the United States, most of them earmarked for the Pacific, were rushed to Europe, and the United States was left without a strategic reserve. In May 1945 the overall ground army numbered 68 infantry, 16 armored, and 5 airborne divisions.

The extent to which the Army depended on its air arm to confer striking power and mobility is suggested by the enormous growth of the Army Air Forces — from about 400,000 men at the beginning of

1942 to a peak of over 2.4 million early in 1944. At the end of the war in Europe it had 243 organized groups in being, and a numerical strength of 2.3 million men. More than 1.5 million of the worldwide AAF strength in March 1945 consisted of service troops, troops in training, and overhead.

After 1942 the growth of the ground army also was very largely in services and administrative elements. By March 1945 these comprised 2.1 million (not counting hospital patients and casuals en route) of the ground army's 5.9 million personnel. This growth reflected both the global character of the war, with its long lines of communications, and the immense numbers of noncombatant specialists needed to operate and service the equipment of a modern mechanized army. They were a manifestation, too, of the American people's insistence on providing the American citizen soldier with something like his accustomed standard of living. Less tangible and more difficult to control was the demand for large administrative and co-ordinating staffs, a demand that was self-generating since administrators themselves had to be administered and co-ordinators co-ordinated. One of the most conspicuous phenomena of global war was the big headquarters. In the European theater in 1944 "overhead" personnel, largely in higher headquarters, numbered some 114,000 men. On the eve of V-E Day, with overseas deployment for the two-front war complete, almost 1.3 million of the 2.8 million men who remained in the United States were in War Department, AGF, ASF, and AAF overhead agencies to operate the Zone of Interior establishment.

The demand for noncombatant personnel was swelled by the assignment to the Army of various administrative tasks. One was the administration of military lend-lease. Another was the development of the atomic bomb, the supersecret, $2 billion Manhattan Project assigned to the Corps of Engineers. Two of the Army's overseas commands — the China-Burma-India Theater and the Perisan Gulf Command — had missions that were largely logistical in character. From the first the Pacific theaters generated the heaviest demands for service troops, to build, operate, and service the manifold facilities needed by a modern army in regions where these were virtually nonexistent. To a lesser degree these needs were also present in the Mediterranean, and operations against the Germans everywhere involved the task of repairing the ruin wrought by the

72

enemy. Big construction projects like the Alcan Highway (from western Canada to Alaska) and the Ledo Road in Burma added to the burden. To carry out the Army's vast procurement program — to compute requirements, negotiate contracts, and expedite production — called for a multitude of highly trained administrators, mostly civilian businessmen whom the Army put into uniform.

Thus, for every three fighting men in the ground army, there were two technicians and administrators somewhere behind, engaged in functions other than killing the enemy. Behind the fighting front, too, stretched the "pipeline," filled with what General McNair once called "the invisible horde of people going here and there but seemingly never arriving." In March 1945 casuals en route or in process of assignment numbered 300,000. Far more numerous were the replacements, who at this time totaled 800,000 in the ground army; AAF replacements numbered 300,000. Almost no provision had been made for replacements in the early troop basis. The necessity of providing spaces for them, as well as for larger numbers of service and AAF troops, in the Army's total allotment of manpower went far to account for the difference between the 215 divisions in the original Victory Program and the 89 actually organized.

Replacements kept the effective strength of the Army from declining. The number of soldiers in hospitals in World War II seldom fell below 200,000, and at the beginning of 1945 reached a peak of almost 500,000. Throughout the war, the Army suffered a total of 936,000 battle casualties, including 235,000 dead; to the latter must be added 83,400 nonbattle deaths. The Army's dead represented about 3 percent of the 10,420,000 men who served in its ranks during World War II.

Despite the acknowledged primacy of the European war, only gradually did the flow of American troops overseas take the direction desired by the Army planners. Not until OVERLORD was given top priority at the Tehran Conference at the end of 1943 could the double war finally begin to assume the focus and flow into the channels planned by the War Department in the early stages of the coalition war. During 1943 the Army sent overseas close to 1.5 million men, including 13 divisions. Over two-thirds of these totals, including more than 1 million troops and 9 divisions, were deployed against Germany. In these terms the balance was finally being

73

redressed in favor of the war against Germany. The cumulative totals at the end of 1943 showed 1.4 million men, including 17 divisions, deployed against Germany, as opposed to 913,000 troops, including 13 divisions, lined up against Japan — a sharp contrast to the picture at the end of 1942, when in manpower and number of divisions the war against Japan had maintained an edge over the war in Europe.

On the other hand, the failure of the Allies to agree on a specific plan for the cross-Channel attack until Tehran permitted deployment in the war against Japan to develop at a much quicker pace than the planners had expected. It was not until October 1943 that the divisions in Europe exceeded those in the Pacific. And when the effort expended by the Navy and Marine Corps, especially in the Pacific, is added to Army deployment overseas, a different picture emerges. Actually, after two years of war, the balance of U.S. forces — and resources — between the European and Japanese arenas was fairly even. Indeed, of the total of 3.7 million men — Army, Navy, and Marines — overseas during 1943, slightly more than half were arrayed against Japan. By the close of that year the growing costs of fighting a multifront war on an opportunistic basis and the difficulty of keeping a secondary war secondary in the absence of a firm long-range plan for the primary war had been driven home to the Army planners.

By the end of the midwar period — in September 1944 — General Marshall and his staff could survey the state of Army deployment with considerable satisfaction. Channeling U.S. military power to the United Kingdom for a concentrated attack against Germany had been a long struggle. More divisions were sent overseas in the first nine months of 1944 — the bulk of them going to the European theater — than had been shipped overseas during the previous two years. To support OVERLORD and its follow-up operations, the Army funneled forces into the European theater and later into continental Europe in ever-increasing numbers during the first three quarters of 1944. Slightly over 2 million men, including 34 divisions and 103 air groups, were in the European theater at the end of September 1944 — over 45 percent of the total number of troops overseas in all Theaters. By then, the overall breakdown of Army troops overseas gave the war against Germany a 2 to 1 advantage over the Japanese conflict, and this was matched by the Army divisional distribution. Forty divisions were located in Europe and the Mediterranean, with 4 more en route, against 21 in the Pacific. In the air, the preponderance lay even more heavily in favor of Europe. With the bulk of the Army's combat strength overseas deployed against the Reich, and with most of the divisions that were in the United States slated to go to the European theater, General Marshall and his planners could consider their original concept well on the way to accomplishment. Although there were still over 3.5 million men left in the continental United States at the end of September, there were only 24 combat divisions remaining. The Army planners had hoped to maintain some of the divisions as a strategic reserve to cope with emergencies.

When the crisis caused by the Ardennes breakthrough of December 1944 denuded the United States of all the remaining divisions, the possibility of having raised too few divisions caused War Department leaders from Stimson on down some anxious moments. Fortunately this was the last unpleasant surprise; another such crisis would have found the divisional cupboard bare. Indeed, the decision for 90 divisions — the Army's "cutting edge" — was one of the greatest gambles taken by the Washington high command in World War II.

Thus, in the long run, Marshall and his staff were not only able to reverse the trend toward the Pacific that had lasted well into 1943 but had gone to the other extreme during 1944. Because of unexpected developments in the European war, not one division was sent to the Pacific after August 1944, and planning deployment totals for the Pacific for 1944 were never attained. European deployment, on the other hand, mounted steadily and substantially exceeded the planners' estimates. At the end of April 1945, when the Army reached its peak strength of 5.4 million overseas, over 3 million were in the European theater and 1.2 million in the Pacific. Regardless of the type of war fought in World War II — concentration and invasion in Europe, or blockade, bombardment, and island hopping in the Pacific — each required a tremendous outlay of American military strength and resources.

Balancing Means and Ends

Throughout the conflict the matching of means with ends, of logistics with strategy, continued to be a complex process, for World War II was the greatest coalition effort and the first really global war in which the United States had been involved. The wherewithal had to be produced and delivered to a multitude of allies and to far-flung fronts over long sea lines of communications and all somehow harnessed to some kind of strategic design to defeat the enemies. As the war progressed, the Army strategic planners learned to appreciate more and more the limits of logistics in the multifront war. From the standpoint of the Americans, the basic strategic decisions they supported from the beginning — the Germany-first decision and the primacy of the cross-Channel attack — were in large measure justified by logistics. Each would capitalize on the advantages of concentrating forces and material resources on a single major line of communications and link the major arsenal represented by the United States with the strategically located logistical base offered by Great Britain. The realities of logistics had in part defeated their original BOLERO strategy, and forces and resources in being in other theaters had generated their own offensive strategy.

In the midwar era, while Allied plans remained unsettled, the competing claims of the Pacific and Mediterranean for a strategy of opportunism, the continuing needs of other far-flung fronts, added to the accumulated "fixed charges" — for example, aid to China, Britain, and the Soviet Union and the rearming of the French — took a heavy toll of American resources. The full-blown war economy was matched by the full-blown war on the global scale. In and out of the international conferences of midwar in the era of relative plenty, the adjustment of means and ends went on and logistics remained a limiting, if not always the final determining, factor in the strategic debate. The scope, timing, landing places, and even the choice of specific operations were to a large extent influenced by the availability of the wherewithal, by the quantities that could be produced and delivered to the fighting fronts.

To logisticians in World War II, the balance among supplies and equipment, trained troops, and the shipping to transport them —

the only means then feasible for mass movement overseas — was of continuing concern. In planning for that balance the factor of lead time was particularly important. For example, for the invasion of Normandy in June 1944 planning for the production of material had to start two years in advance, the buildup in England at least a year in advance, and the actual planning of detailed logistical support six months before the landings. Usually the shorter the lead time for logistical preparations, the narrower the range of strategic choices tended to be.

To the end the Army was, of course, one cog in the mighty American war machine, and it had to compete for resources with its sister services and with allies. The home front, too, had to be supported. While the war cut deeply into the life of the American people, it was fought with a "guns and butter" policy without any real sacrifice in the American standard of living. The Army was not anxious to cut into that standard of living. Nor did it have final say over the allocation and employment of key resources. To balance the allocation of forces, supplies, and shipping among the many fronts and nations, within the framework of the close partnership with the British, required a degree of central logistical control and direction at both combined and national level unknown in earlier wars. A complex network of Anglo-American and national civilian and military agencies for logistical planning emerged. In the melding of resources and plans that went on in and out of the international conferences, planners took their cue from the basic decisions of the CCS — in this sense, the top logistical as well as strategic planning organization.

An imposing structure of federal agencies and committees grew up in Washington to control the nation's economic mobilization. Its keystone was the influential War Production Board (WPB) that controlled the allocation and use of raw materials, machine tools, and facilities, with powers similar to those of the War Industries Board in World War I. In the military sphere the War Department, like the Navy Department, had a large degree of autonomy in controlling requirements planning, production, and distribution of material for its forces. The actual procurement — that is, purchasing and contracting of munitions and other war materials — was carried out directly by the Army's technical services and the Navy's bureaus. Within the Joint Chiefs of Staff organization many logistical problems at issue between the services were settled by negotiation. The War Shipping Administration (WSA) operated and allocated the critical United States merchant shipping. Close co-operation between WSA and the British Ministry of War Transport resulted in the pooling of the two merchant fleets, comprising the bulk of the world's mercantile tonnage. Other civilian agencies dealt with such critical commodities as food, petroleum products, and rubber. In the spring of 1943 most of the mobilization agencies were subordinated to a new co-ordinating unit, the Office of War Mobilization headed by former Justice James F. Byrnes.

Theoretically U.S. munitions production along with that of the British empire was placed in a "common pool" and distributed according to strategic need. Allocations were made by two Munitions Assignments Boards, each representing both countries and responsible to the CCS. One board, sitting in Washington, allocated U.S. production, while a second in London allocated British production. Using the principles of lend-lease and reciprocal aid, these two boards made allocations to other Western Allied countries as well as to the United States and Britain. Supplies for the Soviet Union were governed by separate diplomatic protocols, and the boards seldom attempted to alter their provisions in making assignments. The common pool theory, however, proved somewhat too idealistic for complete application. It really applied from the start almost entirely to American production, for the British had little surplus to distribute. Their contributions to the American effort, though substantial, normally took the form of services and soft goods rather than military hardware. In these circumstances, the Americans almost inevitably came to question the application of the common pool theory and to make assignments on the premise that each partner had first call on its own resources. British participation in the allocation of American production became only nominal in the later war years.

However imperfect the application of the common pool concept, lend-lease, with its counterpart, reciprocal aid, proved an admirable instrument of coalition warfare. Lend-lease did what President Roosevelt had initially intended it should. It removed the dollar sign from Allied supply transactions and gave the Allies an unprecedented flexibility in distributing materials without generating complicated financial transactions or postwar problems such as the war debts of World War I had created. Under the Lend-Lease Act of March 1941, the War Department turned over to Allied countries approximately $25 billion worth of war materials. About 58 percent went to Britain, 23 percent to Russia, 8 percent to France, 7 percent to China, and the remainder to other countries. Included in these supplies were some 37,000 light and medium tanks, nearly 800,000 trucks, and 3,400 locomotives. The Army Service Forces was the Army's operating agency for administering this program, and from 1942 on military lend-lease requirements were included with U.S. Army requirements in the Army supply program. This American largess was distributed almost exclusively under the principle of achieving complete military victory in the war, not of contributing to the postwar political purposes of any ally.

Even with American production in high gear during 1943-45, critical shortages or bottlenecks developed to hamper operations at various stages. In early 1943, as in 1942, the most stringent limiting factor was ocean shipping to transport troops and supplies overseas. Indeed, in the spring of 1943, when President Roosevelt decided to divert scarce shipping to support the faltering British economy, he had to overrule the JCS, deeply concerned over American military requirements — one of the few occasions in the war he did so. After mid-1943, amid the changing requirements of the war in full bloom, the logistical bottlenecks tended to be specialized rather than general. From late 1943 until June 1944 the most serious critical shortage became the supply of assault shipping to land troops and supplies in amphibious operations. In the case of landing craft, the shortage was most severe in one specific category, the Landing Ship Tank (LST). In April 1944 Winston Churchill became exasperated enough to wonder whether history would ever understand why "the plans of two great empires like Britain and the United States should be so much hamstrung and limited" by an "absurd shortage of the L.S.T.'s." In the last stage, after troops were ashore and fighting on the European continent, the principal bottleneck shifted to port and inland clearance capacity in both that area and in the Pacific.

The basic problem of allocating resources between the war against Germany and the war against Japan remained almost to the end. Although the basic decision of "Germany first" held throughout the conflict, one of the most persistent questions concerned the proportion in which available resources should be divided between

79

LST Discharging Cargo Over a Ponton Causeway, Gela, Sicily

the two wars. This question reflected some divergence of political, military, geographical, and psychological factors in the Anglo-American strategy of the war. For Britain, the war against Japan tended to be a side show, and its leaders tended to emphasize the effort in Europe and the Mediterranean at the expense of the Pacific. The United States more than met its commitments in Europe but insisted from the beginning on a margin of safety in the war against Japan, for which it early had been given major responsibility. Furthermore, the pull to the Pacific in midwar that the U.S. Navy and General MacArthur, both now on the offensive, particularly welcomed became for the Washington high command a lever against overcommitment in the Mediterranean. At the midwar conferences the Anglo-American debate focused on the division of resources among the theaters where the two nations combined their efforts — the Mediterranean, northwest Europe, and Southeast Asia. For the Pacific, American military leaders simply presented their decisions, logistical as well as strategic, to the conferences for the stamp of approval. In effect, American military leaders in midwar went far toward asserting unilateral control over the division of American resources between the two wars.

In the final analysis, the multifront nature of the war developed as a product of changing circumstances rather than of a predetermined grand design. Coalition strategy evolved as a result of a complex, continuing process — a constant struggle to adjust ends and means, to reconcile diverse pressures, pulls, and shifting conditions in the global war, and to effect compromises among nations with diverse national interests. That strategy, frequently dictated by necessity, often emerged from events rather than determined them.

The Washington high command was to end the war as it began it — without a fully developed theory on how to match strategic plans, manpower, and resources for a coalition, global war. But throughout its search for the formula for victory it had consistently pursued its goal of winning the war decisively, of complete military victory, without concern for postwar political aims. Whatever general political objectives the President had, he was committed to no strategic doctrine except complete victory. The political and military spheres of American national policy continued their customary separate ways.

Institutionally, World War II became for American strategists and logisticians an organization war, a war of big planning staffs in the capitals and the theater headquarters. Strategy and logistics became big business — established industries in the huge American wartime military establishment. World War II contributed significantly to the education of American Army planners in these arts. General Marshall, for example, once succinctly observed that his military experience in World War I had been based on roads, rivers, and railroads; in World War II he had to learn all over again and to acquire "an education based on oceans."

Throughout Americans evinced their national habit in war — a penchant for quick, direct, and total solutions. The strategic principles they stressed were entirely in harmony with their own traditions and capacities. They proved particularly adept in adapting

81

their mass-production economy to war purposes and in applying power on a massive scale. How far they had come in the quarter century since World War I was evidenced by a comparison of their strategic experience in the two coalition world wars of the twentieth century. In World War I the United States, a junior partner, conformed to the strategy set by the Allies; in World War II the United States came to hold its own in allied war councils and played an influential role in molding Allied strategy, virtually dictating the strategy of the Pacific war. In meeting the problems of global coalition warfare, in the greatest conflict in which the United States had been involved, American strategists and logisticians came of age.

The multifront war of mass, technology, and mobility that taxed the strategists and logisticians in Washington also challenged the overseas commands and the tacticians in the field. As the war had progressed, the role of the theater commands in strategy, logistics, and tactics had become increasingly significant. It is appropriate, therefore, at this point to turn from Washington high command to the Army overseas and to trace the actual course of operations in the double war.

CHAPTER 4

World War II: The War Against Germany and Italy

With the invasion of North Africa (Operation TORCH), the U.S. Army in late 1942 began a ground offensive against the European Axis that was to be sustained almost without pause until Italy collapsed and Germany was finally defeated. More than a million Americans were to fight in lands bordering the Mediterranean Sea and close to four million on the European continent, exclusive of Italy, in the largest commitment to battle ever made by the U.S. Army. Alongside these Americans were to march British, Canadian, French, and other Allied troops in history's greatest demonstration of coalition warfare, while on another front massed Soviet armies were to contribute enormously to the victory.

The North African Campaign, November 1942-May 1943

Although the decision to launch Operation TORCH had been made largely because the Allies could not mount a more direct attack against the European Axis early in the war, there were specific and attractive objectives — to gain French-controlled Morocco, Algeria, and Tunisia as a base for enlisting the French empire in the war, to assist the British in the Libyan Desert in destroying Axis forces in North Africa, to open the Mediterranean

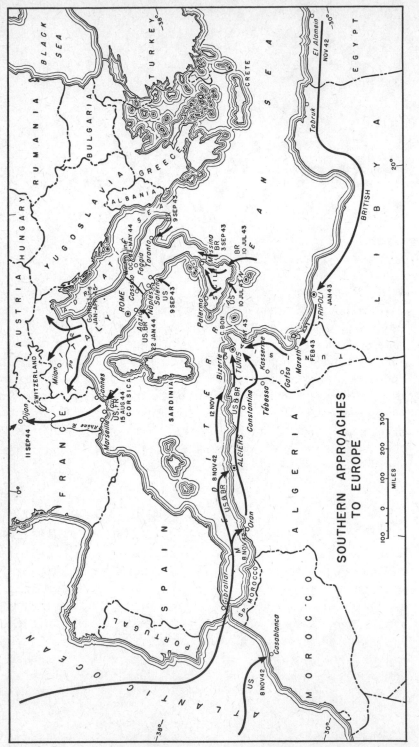

SOUTHERN APPROACHES
TO EUROPE

MAP 1

to Allied shipping, and to provide a steppingstone for subsequent operations.

The Germans and their Italian allies controlled a narrow but strategic strip of the North African littoral between Tunisia and Egypt with impassable desert bounding the strip on the south. (*Map 1*) Numbering some 100,000 men under a battle-tested German leader, Field Marshal Rommel, the German-Italian army in Libya posed a constant threat to Egypt and the Near East as well as to French North Africa and, since the Axis also controlled the northern shores of the Mediterranean, served to deny the Mediterranean to Allied shipping. Only a few convoys seeking to supply British forces on the island of Malta ever ventured into the Mediterranean, and these took heavy losses.

Moving against French Africa posed for the Allies special problems rooted in the nature of the armistice that had followed French defeat in 1940. Under terms of that armistice, the Germans had left the French empire nominally intact, along with much of the southern half of Metropolitan France, yet in return the French Government was pledged to drop out of the war. Although an underground resistance movement had already begun in France and an Allied-equipped force called the Free French was assembling in the British Isles, that part of the regular French Army and Navy left intact by the armistice was sworn to the service of the Vichy government. This pledge had led already to the anomaly of Frenchman fighting Frenchman and of the British incurring French enmity by destroying part of the fleet of their former ally.

If bloodshed was to be averted in the Allied invasion, French sympathies had to be enlisted in advance, but to reveal the plan was to risk French rejection of it and German occupation of French Africa. Although clandestine negotiations were conducted with a few trusted French leaders, these produced no guarantee that French forces would not resist.

Partly because of this intricate situation, the Allies designated an American, General Eisenhower, to command the invasion in order to capitalize on absence of rancor between French and Americans by giving the invasion an American rather than a British complexion. American troops were to make up the bulk of the assault force, and the Royal Navy was to keep its contribution as inconspicuous as possible.

The operation was to begin in western Egypt, where the British Commander in Chief, Middle East, General Sir Harold R. L. G. Alexander, was to attack with the veteran British Eighth Army under Lt. Gen. Bernard L. Montgomery against Field Marshal Rommel's German-Italian army. Coming ashore in French Africa, General Eisenhower's combined U.S.-British force was to launch a converging attack against Rommel's rear.

In selecting beaches for the invasion, U.S. planners insisted upon a landing on the Atlantic coast of Morocco lest the Germans seal the Strait of Gibraltar and cut off support to forces put ashore on the Mediterranean coast. Because both troops and shipping were limited, a landing on the Atlantic coast restricted the number and size of landings possible inside the Mediterranean. Although a landing as far east as Tunisia was desirable because of vast overland distances (from the Atlantic coast to Tunis is more than a thousand miles), proximity of Axis aircraft on Sicily and Sardinia made that too perilous.

Making the decision on the side of security, the Allies planned simultaneous landings at three points — in Morocco near the Atlantic port of Casablanca and in Algeria near the ports of Oran and Algiers. Once the success of these landings was assured, a convoy was to put ashore small contingents of British troops to seize ports in eastern Algeria while a ground column headed for Tunisia in a race to get there before the Germans could move in.

Given the assignment to invade North Africa only at the end of July 1942, the U.S. Army faced enormous difficulties in meeting a target date in November of the same year. Troops had had little training in amphibious warfare, landing craft were few and obsolete, and much equipment was inferior to that of the Axis forces. So few U.S. troops were available in England that troops for the landing near Casablanca had to be shipped direct from the United States, one of history's longest sea voyages preceding an amphibious assault.

After soundly defeating an Axis attack, Montgomery's Eighth Army on October 23 auspiciously opened an offensive at El 'Alamein, there to score a victory that was to be a turning point in British fortunes. A little over two weeks later, before daylight on November 8, the U.S. Navy put U.S. Army forces ashore near Casablanca, while the Royal Navy landed other U.S. troops and contingents of British troops near Oran and Algiers. The entire invasion force consisted of over 400 warships, 1,000 planes, and some 107,000 men, including a battalion of paratroopers jumping in the U.S. Army's first airborne attack.

Although the invasion achieved strategic surprise, the French in every case but one fought back at the beaches. Dissidence among various French factions limited the effectiveness of some of the opposition, but any resistance at all raised the specter of delay that might enable the Germans to beat the Allies into Tunisia. Three days passed before the French agreed to cease fire and take up arms on the Allied side.

French support at last assured, the Royal Navy put British troops ashore close to the Tunisian border while an Allied column began the long overland trek. The British troops were too few to do more than secure two small Algerian ports, the ground column too late. Over the narrow body of water between Sicily and North Africa the Germans poured planes, men, and tanks. Except for barren mountains in the interior, Tunisia was for the moment out of Allied reach.

The Tunisia Campaign

Recoiling from the defeat at El 'Alamein, Rommel's German-Italian army in January 1943 occupied old French fortifications near the southern border of Tunisia, the Mareth Line, there to face Montgomery's Eighth Army, while more than 100,000 enemy troops under General Juergen von Arnim faced westward against General Eisenhower's Allied force. Although the Italian high command in Italy exercised loose control, the Axis nations failed to establish a unified command over these two forces.

The Allied plan to defeat Rommel by converging attacks having been foiled, General Eisenhower had no choice but to dig in to defend in the Tunisian mountains until he could accumulate enough strength to attack in conjunction with a renewed strike by Montgomery against the Mareth Line. Before this could be accomplished, Rommel on February 14 sent strong armored forces through the passes in central Tunisia against the U.S. II Corps, commanded by Maj. Gen. Lloyd R. Fredendall. Rommel planned to push through the Kasserine Pass, then turn northwestward by way of an Allied supply base at Tébessa to reach the coast and trap the Allied units.

In a series of sharp armored actions, Rommel quickly penetrated thinly held American positions and broke through the Kasserine Pass. Although success appeared within his grasp, lack of unified command interfered. Planning an attack of his own, General von Arnim refused to release an armored division needed to continue Rommel's thrust. Concerned that Rommel lacked the strength for a deep envelopment by way of Tébessa, the Italian high command directed a turn northward, a much shallower envelopment.

The turn played into Allied hands, for the British already had established a blocking position astride the only road leading northward. At the height of a clash between Rommel's tanks and the British, four battalions of American artillery arrived after a forced march from Oran. On February 22 these guns and a small band of British tanks brought the Germans to a halt. Warned by intelligence reports that the British Eighth Army was about to attack the Mareth Line, Rommel hurriedly pulled back to his starting point.

The Axis offensive defeated, the U.S. II Corps, commanded now by Maj. Gen. George S. Patton, Jr., launched a diversionary attack on March 17 toward the rear of the Mareth Line, while Montgomery's Eighth Army a few days later struck the line in force. By the end of the first week of April, the two forces had joined.

With all their forces now linked under the tactical command of General Alexander, the Allies opened a broad offensive that within a month captured the ports of Bizerte and Tunis and compressed all Axis troops into a small bridgehead covering the Cape Bon peninsula at the northeastern tip of Tunisia. The last of some 275,000 Germans and Italians surrendered on May 10.

Although the original Allied strategy had been upset by the delay imposed by French resistance and the swift German build-up in Tunisia, Allied troops achieved victory in six months, which in view of their limited numbers and long lines of communications, was impressive. A few days later the first unopposed British convoy since 1940 reached beleaguered Malta.

American troops in their first test against German arms had made many mistakes. Training, equipment, and leadership had failed in many instances to meet the requirements of the battlefield, but the lessons were clear and pointed to nothing that time might not correct. More important was the experience gained, both in battle and in logistical support. Important too was the fact that the Allied campaign had brought a French army back into the war. Most important of all, the Allies at last had gained the initiative.

The Sicily Campaign, July-August 1943

Where the Allies were to go after North Africa had already been decided in January 1943 at the Casablanca Conference. As with the decision to invade North Africa, the next step — invading Sicily (Operation HUSKY) — followed from recognition that the Allies still were unready for a direct thrust across the English Channel. Utilizing troops already available in North Africa, they could make the Mediterranean safer for Allied shipping by occupying Sicily, perhaps going on after that to invade Italy and knock the junior Axis partner out of the war.

As planning proceeded for the new operation, General Eisenhower (promoted now to four-star rank) remained as supreme commander, while General Alexander, heading the 15th Army Group, served as ground commander. Alexander controlled Montgomery's Eighth Army and a newly created Seventh U.S. Army under Patton (now a lieutenant general).

How to invade the Vermont-size, three-cornered island posed a special problem. The goal was Messina, the gateway to the narrow body of water between Sicily and Italy, the enemy's escape route to the Italian mainland. Yet the Strait of Messina was so narrow and well fortified that Allied commanders believed the only solution was to land elsewhere and march on Messina by way of shallow coastal shelves on either side of towering Mount Etna.

Applying the principle of mass, Alexander directed that all landings be made in the southeastern corner of the island, British on the east coast, Americans on the southwest. Behind British beaches a brigade of glider troops was to capture a critical bridge, while a regiment of U.S. paratroopers took high ground behind American beaches. After seizing minor ports and close-in airfields, Patton's Seventh Army was to block to the northwest against Axis reserves while Montgomery mounted a main effort up the east coast.

Because Sicily was an obvious objective after North Africa, complete strategic surprise was hardly possible, but bad weather helped the Allies achieve tactical surprise. As a huge armada bearing some 160,000 men steamed across the Mediterranean, a mistral — a form of unpredictable gale common to the Mediterranean — sprang up, so churning the sea that General Eisenhower was for a time tempted to order delay. While the heavy surf swamped some landing craft and made all landings difficult, it put the beach defenders off their guard. Before daylight on July 10, both British and Americans were ashore in sizable numbers.

As presaged in North Africa, poor performance by Italian units left to German reserves the task of repelling the invasion. Although preattack bombardment by Allied planes and confusion caused by a scattered jump of U.S. paratroopers delayed German reaction, a panzer division mounted a sharp counterattack against American beaches before the first day was out. It came dangerously close to pushing some American units into the sea before naval gunfire and a few U.S. tanks and artillery pieces that had got ashore drove off the German tanks.

To speed reinforcement, the Allies on two successive nights flew in American and British paratroopers. In both instances, antiaircraft gunners on ships standing offshore and others on land mistook the planes for enemy aircraft and opened fire. Losses were so severe that for a time some Allied commanders questioned the wisdom of employing this new method of warfare.

The Germans meanwhile formed a solid block in front of the British along the east coast, prompting General Patton to urge expanding the role of his Seventh Army. First cutting the island in two with a drive by the II Corps, commanded now by Maj. Gen. Omar N. Bradley, Patton sent a provisional corps pushing rapidly through faltering Italian opposition to the port of Palermo and the northwestern tip of the island. This accomplished within fourteen days after coming ashore, Patton turned to aid the British by attacking toward Messina along a narrow northern coastal shelf.

As both Allied armies in early August readied a final assault to gain Messina, the Germans began to withdraw to the mainland. Despite Allied command of sea and air, they managed to evacuate all their forces, some 40,000 troops. When on August 17, thirty days after the invasion, U.S. patrols pushed into Messina, the Germans had incurred some 10,000 casualties, the Italians probably as many as 100,000, mostly prisoners of war. Allied losses were 22,000.

The American force that fought in Sicily was far more sophisticated than that which had gone into battle in North Africa. New landing craft, some capable of bearing tanks, had made getting ashore much quicker and surer, and new amphibious trucks called DUKW's eased the problem of supply over the beaches. Gone was the Grant tank with its side-mounted gun, lacking wide traverse; in its place was the Sherman with 360-degree power-operated traverse for a turret-mounted 75-mm. piece. Commanders were alert to avoid a mistake often made in North Africa of parceling out divisions in small increments, and the men were sure of their weapons and their own ability. Some problems of co-ordination with tactical air remained, but these soon would be worked out.

The Surrender of Italy

Even as the Allies had been preparing to invade Sicily, the Italian people and their government had become increasingly disenchanted with the war. Under the impact of the loss of North Africa, the invasion of Sicily, and a first bombing of Rome, the Italian king forced Mussolini to resign as head of the government.

Anxious to find a way out of the war, a new Italian government made contact with the Allies through diplomatic channels, leading to direct talks with General Eisenhower's representatives. The Italians, it soon developed, were in a quandary — they wanted to pull out of the war, yet they were virtual prisoners of German forces in Italy that Hitler, sensing Italian defection, strongly reinforced. Although plans were drawn for airborne landings to secure Rome coincident with announcement of Italian surrender, these were canceled in the face of Italian vacillation and inability to guarantee strong assistance in fighting the Germans. The Italian government nevertheless agreed to surrender, a fact General Eisenhower announced on the eve of the principal Allied landing on the mainland.

91

The Italian Campaign, September 1943-May 1945

Since the Allied governments had decided to pursue after Sicily whatever course offered the best chance of knocking Italy from the war, invading the mainland logically followed. This plan also presented an opportunity to tie down German forces and prevent their employment either on the Russian front or against the eventual Allied attack across the English Channel. Occupying Italy also would provide airfields close to Germany and the Balkans.

How far up the peninsula of Italy the Allies were to land depended almost entirely on the range of fighter aircraft based on Sicily, for all Allied aircraft carriers were committed to the war in the Pacific. Another consideration was a desire to control the Strait of Messina to shorten sea supply lines.

On September 3 a British force under Montgomery crossed the Strait of Messina and landed on the toe of the Italian boot against surprisingly moderate opposition. Following Eisenhower's announcement of Italian surrender, a British fleet steamed brazenly into the harbor of Taranto in the arch of the Italian boot to put a British division ashore on the docks, while the Fifth U.S. Army under Lt. Gen. Mark W. Clark staged an assault landing on beaches near Salerno, twenty-five miles southeast of Naples.

Reacting in strength against the Salerno invasion, the Germans two days after the landing mounted a vigorous counterattack that threatened to split the beachhead and force abandonment of part of it. For four days, the issue was in doubt. Quick reinforcement of the ground troops (including a regiment of paratroopers jumping into the beachhead), gallant fighting, liberal air support, and unstinting naval gunfire at last repulsed the German attack. On September 15 the Germans began to withdraw, and the next day patrols of the British Eighth Army arrived from the south to link the two Allied forces. Two weeks later American troops took Naples, thereby gaining an excellent port, while the British seized valuable airfields around Foggia on the other side of the peninsula.

Although the Germans seriously considered abandoning southern Italy to pull back to a line in the Northern Apennines, the local commander, Field Marshal Albert Kesselring, insisted that he could hold for a considerable time on successive lines south of Rome. This proved to be an accurate assessment. The Allied advance was destined to proceed slowly, partly because of the difficulty of offensive warfare in rugged mountainous terrain and partly because the Allies limited their commitment to the campaign, not only in troops but also in shipping and the landing craft that were necessary if the enemy's strong defensive positions were to be broken by other than frontal attack.

Because the build-up for a cross-Channel attack — the main effort against Germany — was beginning in earnest, the Allies could spare few additional troops or shipping to pursue the war in Italy. Through the fall and winter of 1943-44, the armies would have to do the job in Italy with what was at hand, a total of eighteen Allied divisions.

A renewed offensive in October 1943 broke a strong German delaying position at the Volturno River, twenty miles north of Naples, and carried as far as a so-called Winter Line, an imposing position anchored on towering peaks around the town of Cassino. Casting about for a way to break this line, General Eisenhower obtained permission to retain temporarily from the build-up in Britain enough shipping and landing craft to make an amphibious end run. General Clark was to use a corps of his Fifth U.S. Army to land on beaches near Anzio, some thirty miles south of Rome and sixty miles behind the Winter Line. By threatening or cutting German lines of communications to the Winter Line, the troops at Anzio were to facilitate Allied advance through the line and up the valley of the Liri River, the most obvious route to Rome.

Provided support by a French corps equipped with American arms, General Clark pulled out the U.S. VI Corps under Maj. Gen. John P. Lucas to make the envelopment. While the VI Corps — which included a British division — sailed toward Anzio, the Fifth Army launched a massive attack aimed at gaining access to the Liri valley. Although the VI Corps landed unopposed at Anzio on January 22, 1944, the attack on the Winter Line gained little.

Rushing reserves to Anzio, Field Marshal Kesselring quickly erected a firm perimeter about the Allied beachhead and successfully resisted every attempt at breakout. On February 16 Kesselring launched a determined attack to eliminate the beachhead that only a magnificent defense by U.S. and British infantry supported by artillery, tanks, planes, and naval gunfire at last thwarted.

93

Through the rest of the winter and early spring, the Fifth and Eighth Armies regrouped and built their combined strength to twenty-five divisions, mainly with the addition of French and British Commonwealth troops. General Eisenhower, meanwhile, had relinquished command in the Mediterranean early in January to go to Britain in preparation for the coming invasion of France. He was succeeded by a Britisher, Field Marshal Sir Henry M. Wilson.

On May 11 the Fifth and Eighth Armies launched a new carefully synchronized attack to break the Winter Line. Passing through almost trackless mountains, French troops under General Clark's command scored a penetration that unhinged the German position. As the Germans began to fall back toward Rome, the VI Corps attacked from the Anzio beachhead but failed to make sufficient progress to cut the enemy's routes of withdrawal. On June 4, 1944, U.S. troops entered Rome.

With D-day in Normandy only two days off, the focus of the Allied war against Germany shifted to France, and with the shift came a gradual diminution of Allied strength in Italy. Allied forces nevertheless continued to pursue the principle of the offensive. Reaching a new German position in the Northern Apennines, the Gothic Line, they started in August a three-month campaign that achieved penetrations, but they were unable to break out of the mountains. This period also saw a change in command as General Clark became commander of the Allied army group and Lt. Gen. Lucian K. Truscott assumed command of the Fifth Army.

In the spring of 1945 the Fifth and Eighth Armies penetrated a final German defensive line to enter the fertile plains of the Po River valley. On May 2, the Germans in Italy surrendered, the first formal capitulation of the war.

Less generally acclaimed than other phases of World War II, the campaign in Italy nevertheless had a vital part in the overall conduct of the war. At the crucial time of the Normandy landings, Allied troops in Italy were tying down twenty-six German divisions that well might have upset the balance in France. As a result of this campaign, the Allies obtained airfields useful for strategic bombardment of Germany and the Balkans, and conquest of the peninsula further guaranteed the safety of Allied shipping in the Mediterranean.

A GERMAN TRENCH ON THE GOTHIC LINE, overlooking a circling road

Cross-Channel Attack

Even as the Allied ground campaign was proceeding on the shores of the Mediterranean, three other campaigns were under way from the British Isles — the campaign of the U.S. Navy and the Royal Navy to defeat the German submarine, a U.S.-British strategic bombing offensive against Germany, and a third, intricately tied in with the other two, a logistical marathon to assemble the men and tools necessary for a direct assault against the foe.

Most critical of all was the antisubmarine campaign, for without success in that, the two others could progress only feebly at best. The turning point in that campaign came in April 1943, when the full effect of all the various devices used against the U-boat began to

95

be apparent. Despite German introduction of an acoustical torpedo that homed on the noise of an escort's propellers, and later of the *schnorkel,* a steel tube extending above water by means of which the U-boat could charge its batteries without surfacing, Allied shipping losses continued to decline. In the last two years of the war the submarines would sink only one-seventh of the shipping they did in the earlier years.

In the second campaign, the combined bomber offensive that U.S. and British chiefs at Casablanca had directed, the demands of the war in the Pacific and the Mediterranean slowed American participation. Not until the summer of 1943 were sufficient U.S. bombers available in Britain to make a substantial contribution, and not until February 1944 were U.S. airmen at last able to match the big thousand-plane raids of the British.

While the Royal Air Force struck by night, bombers of the U.S. Army Air Forces hit by day, both directing much of their attention to the German aircraft industry in an effort to cripple the German air arm before the invasion. Although the raids imposed delays on German production, the most telling effect was the loss of German fighter aircraft and trained pilots rising to oppose the Allied bombers. As time for the invasion approached, the German air arm had ceased to represent a real threat to Allied ground operations, and Allied bombers could shift their attention to transportation facilities in France in an effort to restrict the enemy's ability to move reserves against the invasion.

The logistical build-up in the British Isles, meanwhile, had been progressing at an ever-increasing pace, easily the most tremendous single logistical undertaking of all time. The program entailed transporting some 1,600,000 men across the submarine-infested Atlantic before D-day and providing for their shelter, hospitalization, supply, training, and general welfare. Mountains of weapons and equipment, ranging from locomotives and big bombers to dental fillings, also had to be shipped.

Planning for the invasion had begun long before as the British, standing alone, looked to the day when they might return to the Continent. Detailed planning began in 1943 when the Combined Chiefs of Staff appointed a Britisher, Lt. Gen. Frederick E. Morgan, as chief of staff to a supreme commander yet to be named. Under Morgan's direction, British and American officers drew up

GENERAL EISENHOWER TALKING TO PARATROOPERS before their drop
behind the normandy beaches

plans for several contingencies, one of which, Operation OVER-
LORD, anticipated a large-scale assault against a still powerful
German Army. This plan served as the basis for a final plan developed early in 1944 after General Eisenhower, designated as the
supreme commander, arrived in Britain and established his
command, Supreme Headquarters, Allied Expeditionary Force, or
SHAEF.

The over-all ground commander for the invasion was the former
head of the British Eighth Army, General Montgomery, who also
commanded the 21 Army Group, the controlling headquarters for
the two Allied armies scheduled to make the invasion. The British
Second Army under Lt. Gen. Sir Miles C. Dempsey was to assault
on the left; the First U.S. Army under Bradley (promoted now to
lieutenant general) on the right.

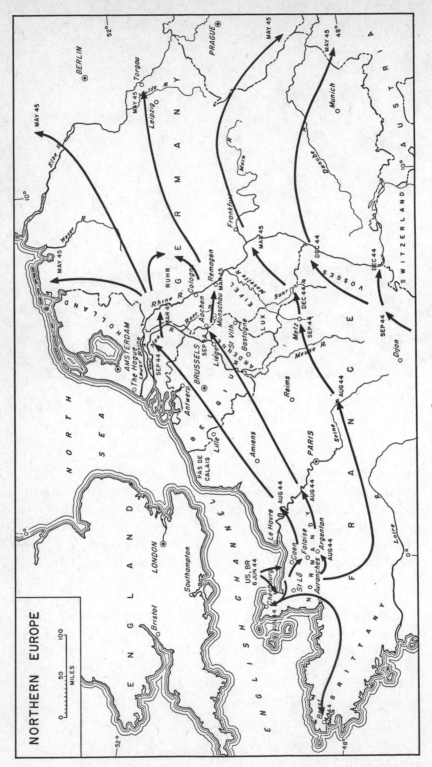

MAP 2

U. S. Troops Moving Ashore at Omaha Beach on D-Day

A requirement that the invasion beaches had to be within easy range of fighter aircraft based in Britain and close to at least one major port sharply limited the choice. The state of German defenses imposed further limitations, leaving only one logical site, the base of the Cotentin peninsula in Normandy, southeast of Cherbourg. (*Map 2*) To facilitate supply until Cherbourg or some other port could be opened, two artificial harbors were to be towed from Britain and emplaced off the invasion beaches.

Despite a weather forecast of high winds and a rough sea, General Eisenhower made a fateful decision to go ahead with the invasion on June 6. During the night over 5,000 ships moved to assigned positions, and at two o'clock, the morning of the 6th, the operation for which the world had long and anxiously waited opened. One British and two U.S. airborne divisions (the 82d and 101st) dropped behind the beaches to secure routes of egress for the seaborne forces. Following preliminary aerial and naval bombardment, the first waves of infantry and tanks began to touch down at 6:30, just after sunrise. A heavy surf made the landings difficult but, as in Sicily, put the defenders off their guard.

The assault went well on British beaches, where one Canadian and two British divisions landed, and also at UTAH, westernmost of the U.S. beaches, where the 4th Division came ashore. The story was different at OMAHA Beach; there an elite German division occupying high bluffs laced with pillboxes put the landings in jeopardy. Allied intelligence had detected the presence of the enemy division too late to alter the landing plan. Only through improvisation and personal courage were the men of two regiments of the 1st Division and one of the 29th at last able to work their way up the bluffs and move slowly inland. Some 50,000 U.S. troops nevertheless made their way ashore on the two beaches before the day was out. American casualties were approximately 6,500, British and Canadian, 4,000 — in both cases lighter than expected.

The German command was slow to react to the invasion, having been misled not only by the weather but also by an Allied deception plan which continued to lead the Germans to believe that this was only a diversionary assault, that the main landings were to come later on the Pas de Calais. Only in one instance, against the British who were solidly ashore, did the Germans mount a sizable counterattack on D-day.

Build-up and Breakout

While Allied aircraft and French resistance fighters impeded the movement of German reserves, the Allies quickly built up their strength and linked the beachheads. U.S. troops then moved against Cherbourg, taking the port, after bitter fighting, three weeks following the invasion. Other Allied forces had in the meantime been deepening the beachhead between Caen and the road center of St. Lô, so that by the end of June the most forward positions were twenty miles from the sea, and the Germans still had been able to mount no major counterattack.

Commanded by Field Marshal Gerd von Rundstedt, the Germans nevertheless defended tenaciously in terrain ideally suited to the defense. This was hedgerow country, where through the centuries French farmers had erected high banks of earth around every small field to fence livestock and protect crops from coastal winds. These banks were thick with the roots of shrubs and trees, and in many places sunken roads screened by a canopy of tree branches ran between two hedgerows. Tunneling into the hedgerows and using the sunken roads for lines of communication, the Germans turned each field into a small fortress.

For all the slow advance and lack of ports (a gale on June 19 demolished one of the artificial harbors and damaged the other), the Allied build-up was swift. By the end of June close to a million men had come ashore, along with some 586,000 tons of supplies and 177,000 vehicles. General Bradley's First Army included four corps with 2 armored and 11 infantry divisions. British strength was about the same.

Seeking to end the battle of the hedgerows, the British attempted to break into more open country near Caen, only to be thwarted by concentrations of German armor. General Bradley then tried a breakout on the right near St. Lô. Behind an intensive aerial bombardment that utilized both tactical aircraft and heavy bombers, the First Army attacked on July 25. By the second day American troops had opened a big breach in German positions, whereupon armored divisions drove rapidly southward twenty-five miles to Avranches at the base of the Cotentin peninsula. While the First Army turned southeastward, the Third U.S. Army under General Patton entered the line to swing through Avranches into Brittany in quest of ports.

The arrival of the Third Army signaled a major change in command. General Bradley moved up to command the 12th Army Group, composed of the First and Third Armies, while his former deputy, Lt. Gen. Courtney H. Hodges, assumed command of the First Army. Montgomery's 21 Army Group consisted of the British Second Army and a newcomer to the front, the First Canadian Army under Lt. Gen. Henry D. G. Crerar. General Montgomery continued to function as overall ground commander, an arrangement that was to prevail for another five weeks until General Eisenhower moved his headquarters to the Continent and assumed direct command of the armies in the field.

In terms of the preinvasion plan, General Eisenhower intended establishing a solid lodgment area in France extending as far east as

101

the Seine River to provide room for air and supply bases. Having built up strength in this area, he planned then to advance into Germany on a broad front. Under Montgomery's 21 Army Group, he would concentrate his greatest resources north of the Ardennes region of Belgium along the most direct route to the Ruhr industrial region, Germany's largest complex of mines and industry. Bradley's 12th Army Group, meanwhile, was to make a subsidiary thrust south of the Ardennes to seize the Saar industrial region along the Franco-German frontier. A third force invading southern France in August was to provide protection on Bradley's right.

The First Army's breakout from the hedgerows changed that plan, for it opened the German armies in France to crushing defeat. When the Germans counterattacked toward Avranches to try to cut off leading columns of the First and Third Armies, other men of the First Army held firm, setting up an opportunity for exploiting the principle of maneuver to the fullest. While the First Canadian Army attacked toward Falaise, General Bradley directed mobile columns of both the First and Third Armies on a wide encircling maneuver in the direction of Argentan, not far from Falaise. This caught the enemy's counterattacking force in a giant pocket. Although a 15-mile gap between Falaise and Argentan was closed only after many of the Germans escaped, more than 60,000 were killed or captured in the pocket. Great masses of German guns, tanks, and equipment fell into Allied hands.

While the First Army finished the business at Argentan, Patton's Third Army dashed off again toward the Seine River, with two objects: eliminating the Seine as a likely new line of German defense and making a second, wider envelopment to trap those German troops that had escaped from the first pocket. Both Patton accomplished. In the two pockets the enemy lost large segments of two field armies.

Invasion of Southern France

Even as General Eisenhower's armies were scoring a great victory in Normandy, the Allies on August 15 staged another invasion, this one in southern France (Operation DRAGOON) to provide a supplementary line of communications through the French Mediterranean ports and to prevent the Germans in the south from moving against the main Allied armies in the north. Lack of landing craft had precluded launching this invasion at the same time as OVERLORD.

Under control of the Seventh U.S. Army, commanded now by Lt. Gen. Alexander M. Patch, three U.S. divisions, plus an airborne task force and French commandos, began landing just after dawn. Defending Germans were spread too thin to provide much more than token resistance, and by the end of the first day the Seventh Army had 86,000 men and 12,000 vehicles ashore. The next day French troops staged a second landing and moved swiftly to seize the ports of Toulon and Marseille.

Faced with entrapment by the spectacular Allied advances in the north, the Germans in southern France began on August 17 to withdraw. U.S. and French columns followed closely and on September 11 established contact with Patton's Third Army. Under the 6th Army Group, commanded by Lt. Gen. Jacob L. Devers, the Seventh Army and French forces organized as the 1st French Army passed to General Eisenhower's command.

Pursuit to the Frontier

As Allied columns were breaking loose all over France, men and women of the French resistance movement began to battle the Germans in the streets of the capital. Although General Eisenhower had intended to bypass Paris, hoping to avoid heavy fighting in the city and to postpone the necessity of feeding the civilian population, he felt impelled to send help lest the uprising be defeated. On August 25 a column including U.S. and French troops entered the city.

With surviving German forces falling back in defeat toward the German frontier, General Eisenhower abandoned the original plan of holding at the Seine while he opened the Brittany ports and established a sound logistical base. Determined to take advantage of the enemy's defeat, he reinforced Montgomery's 21 Army Group by sending the First U.S. Army close alongside the British, thus providing enough strength in the northern thrust to assure quick capture of ports along the English Channel, particularly the great

Belgian port of Antwerp. Because the front was fast moving away from Brittany, the Channel ports were essential.

Ports posed a special problem, for with the stormy weather of fall and winter approaching, the Allies could not much longer depend upon supply over the invasion beaches, and Cherbourg had only a limited capacity. Even though Brittany now was far behind the advancing front, General Eisenhower still felt a need for the port of Brest. He put those troops of the Third Army that had driven into the peninsula under a new headquarters, the Ninth U.S. Army commanded by Lt. Gen. William H. Simpson, and set them to the task. When Brest fell two weeks later, the port was a shambles. The port problem nevertheless appeared to be solved when on September 4 British troops took Antwerp, its wharves and docks intact; but the success proved to be illusory. Antwerp is on an estuary sixty miles from the sea, and German troops clung to the banks, denying access to Allied shipping.

The port situation was symptomatic of multitudinous problems that had begun to beset the entire Allied logistical apparatus (organized much like Pershing's Services of Supply, but called the Communications Zone). The armies were going so far and so fast that the supply services were unable to keep pace. Although enough supplies were available in Normandy, the problem was to get them to forward positions that sometimes were more than 500 miles beyond the depots. Despite extraordinary measures such as establishing a one-way truck route called the Red Ball Express, supplies of such essential commodities as gasoline and ammunition began to run short. This was the penalty the Allied armies would have to pay for the decision to make no pause at the Seine.

The logistical crisis sparked a difference over strategy between General Eisenhower and General Montgomery. In view of the logistical difficulties, Montgomery insisted that General Patton's Third Army should halt in order that all transportation resources might be concentrated behind his troops and the First Army. This allocation, he believed, would enable him to make a quick strike deep into Germany and impel German surrender.

Acting on the advice of logistical experts on his staff, General Eisenhower refused. Such a drive could succeed, his staff advised, only if all Allied armies had closed up to the Rhine River and if Antwerp were open to Allied shipping. The only choice, General

Eisenhower believed, was to keep pushing all along the line while supplies held out, ideally to go so far as to gain bridgeheads over the Rhine.

There were obstacles other than supply standing in the way of that goal. Some were natural, like the Moselle and Meuse Rivers, the Vosges Mountains in Alsace, the wooded hills of the Ardennes, and a dense Huertgen Forest facing the First Army near Aachen. Others were man made, old French forts around Metz and the French Maginot Line in northeastern France, as well as dense fortifications all along the German border — the Siegfried Line, or, as the Germans called it, the West Wall. By mid-September the First Army had penetrated the West Wall at several points but lacked the means to exploit the breaks.

Although General Eisenhower assigned first priority to clearing the seaward approaches to Antwerp, he sanctioned a Montgomery proposal to use Allied airborne troops in a last bold stroke to capitalize on German disorganization before logistics should force a halt. While the British Second Army launched an attack called Operation GARDEN, airborne troops of a recently organized First Allied Airborne Army (Lt. Gen. Lewis H. Brereton) were to land in Operation MARKET astride three major water obstacles in the Netherlands — the Maas, Waal, and Lower Rhine Rivers. Crossing these rivers on bridges to be secured by the airborne troops, the Second Army was to drive all the way to the IJssel Meer (Zuider Zee), cutting off Germans farther west and putting the British in a position to outflank the West Wall and drive into Germany along a relatively open north German plain.

Employing one British and two U.S. airborne divisions, the airborne attack began on September 17. On the first day alone approximately 20,000 paratroopers and glider troops landed in the largest airborne attack of the war. Although the drops were spectacularly successful and achieved complete surprise, the chance presence of two panzer divisions near the drop zones enabled the Germans to react swiftly. Resistance to the ground attack also was greater than expected, delaying quick link-up with the airheads. The combined operation gained a salient some fifty miles deep into German-held territory but fell short of the ambitious objectives, including a bridgehead across the Lower Rhine.

At this point, Montgomery (promoted now to field marshal)

105

concentrated on opening Antwerp to Allied shipping, but so determined was German resistance and so difficult the conditions of mud and flood in the low-lying countryside that it was well into November before the job was finished. The first Allied ship dropped anchor in Antwerp only on November 28.

As a result of a cutback in offensive operations and extraordinary efforts of the supply services, the logistical situation had been gradually improving. In early November resources were sufficient to enable the U.S. armies to launch a big offensive aimed at reaching the Rhine; but, despite the largest air attack in direct support of ground troops to be made during the war (Operation QUEEN), it turned out to be a slow, arduous fight through the natural and artificial obstacles along the frontier. Heavy rain and severe cold added to the difficulties. By mid-December the First and Ninth Armies had reached the Roer River east of Aachen, twenty-three miles inside Germany, and the Third Army had come up to the West Wall along the Saar River northeast of Metz, but only the Seventh Army and the 1st French Army in Alsace had touched any part of the Rhine.

Having taken advantage of the pause imposed by Allied logistical problems to create new divisions and rush replacements to the front, the Germans in the west had made a remarkable recovery from the debacle in France. Just how remarkable was soon to be forcefully demonstrated in what had heretofore been a quiet sector held by the First Army's right wing.

The Ardennes Counteroffensive

As early as the preceding August, Adolf Hitler had been contemplating a counteroffensive to regain the initiative in the west and compel the Allies to settle for a negotiated peace. Over the protests of his generals, who thought the plan too ambitious, he ordered an attack by twenty-five divisions, carefully conserved and secretly assembled, to hit thinly manned U.S. positions in the Ardennes region of Belgium and Luxembourg, cross the Meuse River, and push on northwestward to Antwerp. In taking Antwerp, Hitler expected to cut off the British 21 Army Group and the First and Ninth U.S. Armies.

106

FIRST ARMY MEN SETTING UP A 57-MM. ANTITANK GUN

Under cover of inclement winter weather, Hitler concentrated his forces in the forests of the Eifel region, opposite the Ardennes. Before daylight on December 16, the Germans attacked along a 60-mile front, taking the VIII Corps and the south wing of the V Corps by surprise. In most places, German gains were rapid, for the American divisions were either inexperienced or seriously depleted from earlier fighting, and all were stretched thin.

The Germans nevertheless encountered difficulties from the first. Cut off and surrounded, small U.S. units continued to fight. At the northern shoulder of the penetration, divisions of the V Corps refused to budge from the vicinity of Monschau, thereby denying critical roads to the enemy and limiting the width of the penetration. At St. Vith American troops held out for six days to block a vital road center. To Bastogne to the southwest, where an armored detachment served as a blocking force, General Eisenhower rushed an airborne division which never relinquished that communications center even though surrounded. Here Brig. Gen. Anthony C. McAuliffe delivered a terse one-word reply to a German demand for surrender: "Nuts!"

Denied important roads and hampered by air attacks as the weather cleared, the Germans fell a few miles short of even their first objective, the Meuse River. The result after more than a month of hard fighting that cost the Americans 75,000 casualties and the Germans close to 100,000 was nothing but a big bulge in the lines, from which the battle drew its popular name.

Faced with a shortage of infantry replacements during the enemy's counteroffensive General Eisenhower offered Negro soldiers in service units an opportunity to volunteer for duty with the infantry. More than 4,500 responded, many taking reductions in grade in order to meet specified requirements. The 6th Army Group formed these men into provisional companies, while the 12th Army Group employed them as an additional platoon in existing rifle companies. The excellent record established by these volunteers, particularly those serving as platoons, presaged major postwar changes in the traditional approach to employing Negro troops.

Although the counteroffensive had given the Allied command some anxious moments, the gallant stands by isolated units had provided time for the First and Ninth Armies to shift troops against the northern flank of the penetration and for the Third Army to hit the penetration from the south and drive through to beleaguered Bastogne. A rapid shift and change in direction of attack by the Third Army was one of the more noteworthy instances during the war of successful employment of the principle of maneuver.

By the end of January 1945, U.S. units had retaken all lost ground and had thwarted a lesser German attack against the 6th Army Group in Alsace. The Germans having expended irreplaceable reserves, the end of the war in Europe was in sight.

The Russian Campaigns

Much of the hope for an early end to the war rested with tremendous successes of the Soviet armies in the east. Having stopped the invading Germans at the gates of Moscow in late 1941 and at Stalingrad in late 1942, the Russians had made great offensive strides westward in both 1943 and 1944. Only a few days after D-day in Normandy the Red Army had launched a massive offensive which by mid-September had reached East Prussia and the gates of the Polish capital of Warsaw. In January 1945, as U.S. troops eliminated the bulge in the Ardennes, the Red Army started a new drive that was to carry to the Oder River, only forty miles from Berlin.

Far greater masses of troops were employed in the east than in the west over vast distances and a much wider front. The Germans had to maintain more than two million combat troops on the Eastern Front as compared with less than a million on the Western Front. Yet the Soviet contribution was less disproportionate than would appear at first glance, for the war in the east was a one-front ground war, whereas the Allies in the west were fighting on two ground fronts and conducting major campaigns in the air and at sea, as well as making a large commitment in the war against Japan. At the same time, the United States was contributing enormously to the war in Russia through lend-lease — almost $11 billion in materials, including over 400,000 jeeps and trucks, 12,000 armored vehicles (including 7,000 tanks, enough to equip some 20-odd U.S. armored divisions), 14,000 aircraft, and 1.75 million tons of food.

The Final Offensive

Soon after the opening of the Soviet January offensive, the Western Allies began a new drive to reach and cross the Rhine, the last barrier to the industrial heart of Germany. Exhausted by the over-ambitious effort in the Ardennes and forced to shift divisions to oppose the Russians, the Germans had little chance of holding west of the Rhine. Although Field Marshal von Rundstedt wanted to conserve his remaining strength for a defense of the river, Hitler would authorize no withdrawal. Making a strong stand at the Roer River and at places where the West Wall remained intact, the Germans imposed some delay but paid dearly in the process, losing 250,000 troops that could have been used to better advantage on the Rhine.

Falling back behind the river, the Germans had made careful plans to destroy all bridges, but something went amis at the Ludendorff railroad bridge in the First Army's sector at Remagen. On March 7 a task force of the 9th Armored Division found the bridge damaged but passable. Displaying initiative and courage, a company of infantry dashed across. Higher commanders acted promptly to reinforce the foothold.

To the south, a division of the Third Army on March 22 made a surprise crossing of the Rhine in assault boats. Beginning late the next day the 21 Army Group and the Ninth U.S. Army staged a full-dress crossing of the lower reaches of the river, complete with an airborne attack rivaling in its dimensions Operation MARKET. The Third Army then made two more assault crossings, and during the last few days of March both the Seventh Army and the 1st French Army of the 6th Army Group crossed farther upstream. Having expended most of their resources west of the river, the Germans were powerless to defeat any Allied crossing attempt.

As the month of April opened, Allied armies fanned out from the Rhine all along the line with massive columns of armor and motorized infantry. Encircling the Ruhr, the First and Ninth Armies took 325,000 prisoners, totally destroying an entire German army group. Although the Germans managed to rally determined resistance at isolated points, a cohesive defensive line ceased to exist.

Since the Russians were within forty miles of Berlin and apparently would reach the German capital first, General Eisenhower put the main weight of the continuing drive behind U.S. armies moving through central Germany to eliminate a remaining pocket of German industry and to link with the Russians. The 21 Army Group meanwhile sealed off the Netherlands and headed toward the base of the Jutland peninsula, while the 6th Army Group turned southeastward to obviate any effort by the Nazis to make a last-ditch stand in the Alps of southern Germany and Austria.

By mid-April Allied armies in the north and center were building up along the Elbe and Mulde Rivers, an agreed line of contact with the Red Army approaching from the east. First contact came on April 25 near the town of Torgau, followed by wholesale German surrenders all along the front and in Italy.

With Berlin in Soviet hands, Hitler a suicide, and almost every corner of Germany overrun, emissaries of the German Government surrendered on May 7 at General Eisenhower's headquarters in Reims, France. The next day, May 8, was V-E Day, the official date of the end of the war in Europe.

The Situation on V-E Day

As V-E Day came, Allied forces in Western Europe consisted of 4½ million men, including 9 armies (5 of them American — one of which, the Fifteenth, saw action only at the last), 23 corps, 91 divisions (61 of them American), 6 tactical air commands (4 American), and 2 strategic air forces (1 American). The Allies had 28,000 combat aircraft, of which 14,845 were American, and they had brought into Western Europe more than 970,000 vehicles and 18 million tons of supplies. At the same time they were achieving final victory in Italy with 18 divisions (7 of them American).

The German armed forces and the nation were prostrate, beaten to a degree never before seen in modern times. Hardly any organized units of the German Army remained except in Norway, Czechoslovakia, and the Balkans, and these would soon capitulate. What remained of the air arm was too demoralized even for a final suicidal effort, and the residue of the German Navy lay helpless in captured northern ports. Through five years of war, the German armed forces had lost over 3 million men killed, 263,000 of them in the west, since D-day. The United States lost 135,576 dead in Western Europe, while Britain, Canada, France, and other Allies incurred after D-day approximately 60,000 military deaths.

Unlike in World War I, when the United States had come late on the scene and provided only those forces to swing the balance of power to the Allied side, the American contribution to the reconquest of Western Europe had been predominant, not just in manpower but as a true arsenal of democracy. American factories produced for the British almost three times more lend-lease materials than for the Russians, including 185,000 vehicles, 12,000 tanks, and enough planes to equip four tactical air forces, and for the French, all weapons and equipment for 8 divisions and 1 tactical air force, plus partial equipment for 3 more divisions.

Although strategic air power had failed to prove the decisive instrument many had expected, it was a major factor in the Allied victory, as was the role of Allied navies, for without control of the sea lanes, there could have been no build-up in Britain and no amphibious assaults. It was nonetheless true that the application of the power of ground armies finally broke the German ability and will to resist.

111

While the Germans had developed a flying bomb and later a supersonic missile, the weapons with which both sides fought the war were in the main much improved versions of those that had been present in World War I — the motor vehicle, the airplane, the machine gun, indirect fire artillery, the tank. The difference lay in such accouterments as excellent radio communications and in a new sophistication, particularly in terms of mobility, that provided the means for rapid exploitation that both sides in World War I had lacked.

From North Africa to the Elbe, U.S. Army generalship proved remarkably effective. Such field commanders as Bradley, Devers, Clark, Hodges, Patton, Simpson, Patch, and numerous corps and division commanders would stand beside the best that had ever served the nation. Having helped develop Army doctrine during the years between the two great wars, these same men put the theories to battlefield test with enormous success. Some indication of the magnitude of the responsibilities they carried is apparent from the fact that late in the war General Bradley as commander of the 12th Army Group had under his command four field armies, 12 corps, and 48 divisions, more than 1,300,000 men, the largest exclusively American field command in U.S. history.

These commanders throughout displayed a steady devotion to the principles of war. Despite sometimes seemingly insurmountable obstacles of weather, terrain, and enemy concentration, they were consistently able to achieve the mass, mobility, and firepower to avoid a stalemate, maintaining the principles of the objective and the offensive and exploiting the principle of maneuver to the fullest. On many occasions they achieved surprise, most notably in the amphibious assaults and at the Rhine. They were themselves taken by surprise twice, in central Tunisia and in the Ardennes, yet in both cases they recovered quickly. Economy of force was particularly evident in Italy, and simplicity was nowhere better demonstrated than in the Normandy landings, despite a complexity inherent in the size and diversity of the invasion forces. From the first, unity of command was present in every campaign, not just at the tactical level but also in the combined staff system that afforded the U.S. and Britain a unity of command and purpose never approached on the Axis side.

CHAPTER 5

World War II: The War Against Japan

In World War II, for the first time, the United States had to fight a war on two fronts. Though the central strategic principle governing allocation of resources to the two fronts provided for concentrating first on the defeat of the European Axis, on the American side this principle was liberally interpreted, permitting conduct of an offensive war against Japan as well as against Germany in the years 1943-45. The U.S. Fleet, expanding after its initial setback at Pearl Harbor much as the Army had, provided the main sinews for an offensive strategy in the Pacific, although the Army devoted at least one-third of its resources to the Pacific war, even at the height of war in Europe. In sum, the United States proved capable, once its resources were fully mobilized, of successfully waging offensives on two fronts simultaneously — a development the Japanese had not anticipated when they launched their attack on Pearl Harbor.

Japan's Strategy

Japan entered World War II with limited aims and with the intention of fighting a limited war. Its principal objectives were to secure the resources of Southeast Asia and much of China and to establish a "Greater East Asia Co-Prosperity Sphere" under Japanese hegemony. In 1895 and in 1905 Japan had gained important

113

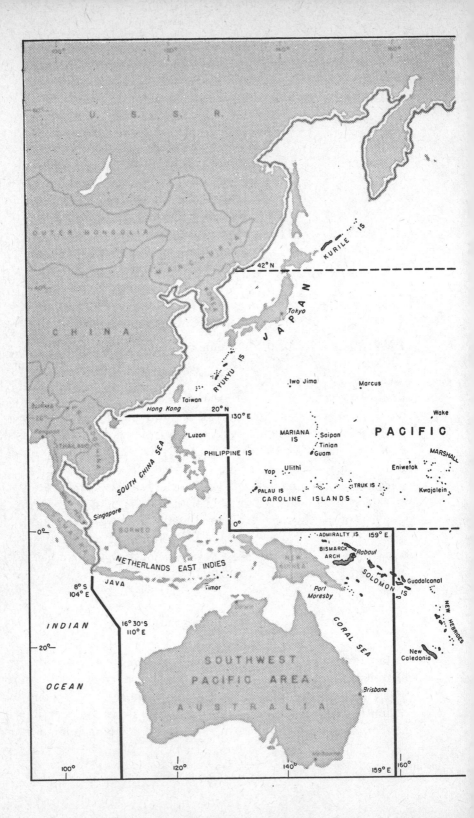

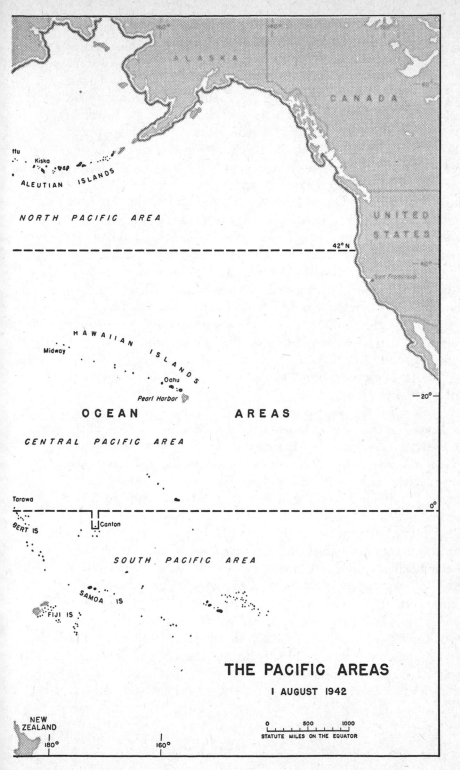

NORTH PACIFIC AREA

ttu
Kiska
ALEUTIAN ISLANDS

42° N

HAWAIIAN ISLANDS
Midway
Oahu
Pearl Harbor

OCEAN   AREAS

CENTRAL PACIFIC AREA

Tarawa

0°

BERT IS
Canton

SOUTH PACIFIC AREA

SAMOA IS
FIJI IS

ALASKA
CANADA
UNITED STATES
San Francisco

20°

THE PACIFIC AREAS

1 AUGUST 1942

NEW
ZEALAND
180°
160°

0   500   1000
STATUTE MILES ON THE EQUATOR

M AP 3

objectives without completely defeating China or Russia and in 1941 Japan sought to achieve its hegemony over East Asia in similar fashion. The operational strategy the Japanese adopted to start war, however, doomed their hopes of limiting the conflict. Japan believed it necessary to destroy or neutralize American striking power in the Pacific — the U.S. Pacific Fleet at Pearl Harbor and the U.S. Far East Air Force in the Philippines — before moving southward and eastward to occupy Malaya, the Netherlands Indies, the Philippines, Wake Island, Guam, the Gilbert Islands, Thailand, and Burma. Once in control of these areas, the Japanese intended to establish a defensive perimeter stretching from the Kurile Islands south through Wake, the Marianas, the Carolines, and the Marshalls and Gilberts to Rabaul on New Britain. From Rabaul the perimeter would extend westward to northwestern New Guinea and would encompass the Indies, Malaya, Thailand, and Burma. Japan thought that the Allies would wear themselves out in fruitless frontal assaults against the perimeter and would ultimately settle for a negotiated peace that would leave it in possession of most of its conquests. (*Map 3*)

The Japanese were remarkably successful in the execution of their offensive plan and by early 1942 had reached their intended perimeter. But they miscalculated the effect of their surprise attack at Pearl Harbor which unified a divided people and aroused the United States to wage a total, not a limited, war. As a result Japan lost, in the long run, any chance of conducting the war on its own terms. The Allies, responding to their defeats, sought no negotiated peace, but immediately began to seek means to strike back. In February and March 1942 small carrier task forces of the Pacific Fleet hit the Marshalls, Wake, and Marcus, and bombers from Australia began to harass the Japanese base at Rabaul. In April Army bombers, flying off a naval carrier, delivered a hit-and-run raid on Tokyo. Meanwhile, the United States began to develop and fortify a line of communications across the southern Pacific to Australia and to strengthen the defenses of the "down-under" continent itself. These new bases, along with Alaska, Hawaii, and India, also strengthened during the period, could become the launching points for counteroffensives. And once the Allies became strong enough to threaten the Japanese defensive perimeter from several directions the Japanese would lose the advantage of interior lines, and with it the strategic initiative, for Japan did not have and could not produce the means to defend and hold at all points.

Perceiving their danger, the Japanese in a second phase offensive tried to sever the Allied lines of communications to Australia and to expand their perimeter in the Pacific. In the spring of 1942 they pushed southeast from Rabaul to Guadalcanal and Tulagi in the Solomons, and seized Attu and Kiska in the Aleutians. But they failed in their main effort to take Midway Island, northwest of Hawaii, and in the naval battles of the Coral Sea and Midway in May and June they lost the bulk of their best naval pilots and planes. Midway was the turning point, for it redressed the naval balance in the Pacific and gave the Allies the strategic initiative. The Japanese, with the mobility of their carrier striking forces curtailed, abandoned plans to cut the Allied South Pacific life line and turned instead to strengthening their defensive perimeter, planning to wage a protracted war of attrition in the hope of securing a negotiated peace.

Guadalcanal and Papua: The First Offensives

After Midway the U.S. Joint Chiefs, responsible for direction of the war in the Pacific, almost naturally turned to the elimination of the threat to their line of communications in the south as the objective of their first offensive. In so doing, they gave to American strategy in the Pacific a twist unanticipated in prewar planning, which had always presupposed that the main offensive in any war against Japan would be made directly across the Central Pacific from Hawaii toward the Philippines. The Joint Chiefs on July 2 directed Allied forces in the South and Southwest Pacific Areas to begin a series of operations aimed at the ultimate reduction of the Japanese stronghold at Rabaul on New Britain Island, thus establishing Allied control of the Bismarck Archipelago.

The campaign would consist of three stages or tasks. In Task One, forces of the South Pacific Area (under Vice Adm. Robert L. Ghormley until November 1942 and thereafter under Admiral William F. Halsey) would seize base sites in the southern Solomons. In Task Two, South Pacific forces would advance up the ladder of the Solomons while Southwest Pacific forces (under

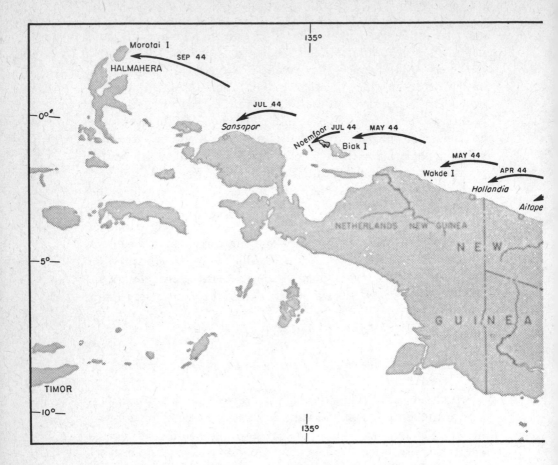

General MacArthur) would move up the north coast of New Guinea as far as Lae and Salamaua. In Task Three, the forces of the two theaters would converge on Rabaul and clear the rest of the Bismarck Archipelago. Task One was to be conducted under the general supervision of Admiral Chester W. Nimitz, whose vast Pacific Ocean Areas command included the North, Central, and South Pacific Areas as subtheaters. Tasks Two and Three would be executed under the strategic direction of General MacArthur. The Joint Chiefs of Staff, reserving to themselves final control of the assignment of tasks, allocation of resources, and timing of operations, would provide, in effect, unified command over Nimitz and MacArthur.

118

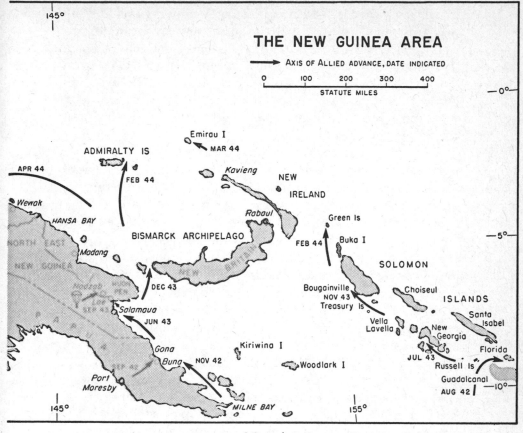

MAP 4

The offensive began on August 7, 1942, when the 1st Marine Division landed on Guadalcanal and nearby islands in the southern Solomons. The Japanese, taking full advantage of interior lines from their bases at Rabaul and Truk, reacted vigorously. Six times from August to the end of November they challenged American naval superiority in the South Pacific in a series of sharp surface engagements. Air battles were almost daily occurrences for a month or more after the landings, and the Japanese sent in strong ground reinforcements, gambling and ultimately losing substantial air and naval resources in the effort to hold Guadalcanal. The Americans had to reinforce heavily, deploying naval power, planes, soldiers, and marines in the battle at the expense of other theaters. Before the

119

island was secured in November, another Marine division (the 2d), two Army divisions (25th and Americal), and one separate regiment, to mention only the major ground combat elements, had been thrown into the battle. The last act came in February 1943, when the 43d Division moved into the Russell Islands, thirty-five miles northwest of Guadalcanal. On Guadalcanal and in the Russells, American forces then began to construct major air and logistical bases for further advances.

A Japanese overland drive toward Port Moresby in New Guinea had meanwhile forced General MacArthur to begin an offensive of his own — the Papua Campaign. (*Map 4*) During the late summer the Japanese had pushed across the towering Owen Stanley Mountains toward Port Moresby from the Buna-Gona area on New Guinea's northeastern coast, and by mid-September were only twenty miles from their objective. Australian ground forces drove the Japanese back to the north coast, where they strongly entrenched themselves around Buna and Gona. It took 2 Australian divisions, 1 U.S. Army division (32d), and another U.S. Army regiment almost four months of bitter fighting to dislodge the Japanese. Casualties were high, but as at Guadalcanal the Allied forces learned much about jungle fighting, the importance of air power, and the need for thorough logistical preparation. They also discovered that the Japanese soldier, though a skillful, stubborn, and fanatic foe, could be defeated. The myth of Japanese invincibility was forever laid to rest in the jungles of Guadalcanal and Papua.

After Papua and Guadalcanal the tempo of operations in the South and Southwest Pacific Areas slowed while General MacArthur and Admiral Halsey gathered resources and prepared based for the next phase. The Japanese, in turn, undertook to reinforce their main bases in New Guinea and the northern Solomons. In March 1943 they attempted to send a large convoy to Lae in New Guinea but, in the Battle of the Bismarck Sea, lost some 3,500 troops and much valuable shipping, principally to Army land-based aircraft. During the following months Rabaul-based planes, reinforced by carrier planes flown in from the Carolines, sought unsuccesfully to knock out American air power in the southern Solomons.

Search for a Strategy

Meanwhile, in the spring and summer of 1943, a strategy for the defeat of Japan began to take shape within Allied councils. The major Allied objective was control of the South China Sea and a foothold on the coast of China, so as to sever Japanese lines of communications southward and to establish bases from which Japan could first be subjected to intensive aerial bombardment and naval blockade and then, if necessary, invaded. The first plans for attaining this objective envisioned Allied drives from several different directions — by American forces across the Pacific along two lines, from the South and Southwest toward the Philippines and from Hawaii across the Central Pacific; and by British and Chinese forces along two other lines, the first a land line through Burma and China and the second a sea line from India via the Netherlands Indies, Singapore, and the Strait of Malacca into the South China Sea. Within the framework of this tentative long-range plan, the U.S. Joint Chiefs fitted their existing plans for completion of the campaign against Rabaul, and a subsequent advance to the Philippines, and developed a plan for the second drive across the Central Pacific. They also, in 1942 and 1943, pressed the Chinese and British to get a drive under way in Burma to reopen the supply line to China in phase with their Pacific advances, offering extensive air and logistical support.

The North Pacific line running from Alaska through the Kuriles to the northernmost Japanese island of Hokkaido also beckoned in early 1943 as a possible additional avenue of approach to Japan. The Joint Chiefs decided, however, that although the Japanese perimeter should be pushed back in this area, the foggy, cold North Pacific with its rock-bound and craggy islands was not a profitable area in which to undertake a major offensive. In May 1943 the U.S. 7th Division went ashore on Attu and, after three weeks of costly fighting through icy muck and over wind-swept ridges in a cold, almost constant fog, destroyed the Japanese garrison. In August a combined American-Canadian expedition landed on Kiska, some distance away, only to find that the Japanese had evacuated the island three weeks earlier. With the Japanese perimeter pushed back to the Kuriles the Allied advance stopped, and further operations were limited to nuisance air raids against these Japanese-held islands. Ground forces used in the attacks on Attu and Kiska were redeployed to the Central Pacific, and some of the defensive forces deployed in Alaska were also freed for employment elsewhere.

Prospects of an advance through China to the coast faded rapidly in 1943. At the Casablanca Conference in January the Combined Chiefs' agreed on an ambitious operation, called ANAKIM, to be launched in the fall of 1943 to retake Burma and reopen the supply line to China. ANAKIM was to include a British amphibious assault on Rangoon and an offensive into central Burma, plus an American-sponsored Chinese offensive in the north involving convergence of forces operating from China and India. ANAKIM proved too ambitious; even limited offensives in Southeast Asia were postponed time and again for lack of adequate resources. By late 1943 the Americans had concluded that their Pacific forces would reach the China coast before either British or Chinese forces could come in through the back door. At the SEXTANT Conference late in 1943 the Combined Chiefs agreed that the main effort against Japan should be concentrated in the Pacific along two lines of advance, with operations in the North Pacific, China, and Southeast Asia to be assigned subsidiary roles.

In this strategy the two lines of advance in the Pacific — the one across the Central Pacific via the Gilberts, Marshalls, Marianas, Carolines, and Palaus toward the Philippines or Formosa (Taiwan) and the other in the Southwest Pacific via the north coast of New Guinea to the Vogelkop and thence to the southern Philippines — were viewed as mutually supporting. (*Map 5*) Although the Joint Chiefs several times indicated a measure of preference for the Central Pacific as the area of main effort, they never established any real priority between the two lines, seeking instead to retain a flexibility that would permit striking blows along either line as opportunity offered. The Central Pacific route promised to force a naval showdown with the Japanese and, once the Marianas were secured, to provide bases from which the U.S. Army Air Forces' new B-29 bombers could strike the Japanese home islands. The Southwest Pacific route was shorter, if existing bases were taken into consideration, and offered more opportunity to employ land-based air power to full advantage. The target area for both drives, in the strategy approved at SEXTANT, was to be the Luzon-Formosa-China coast

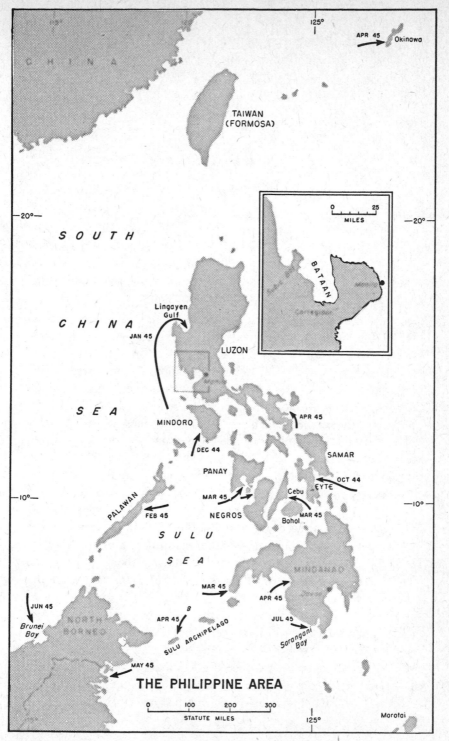

APR 45 → Okinawa

CHINA

TAIWAN
(FORMOSA)

—20°

20°

SOUTH

CHINA

SEA

BATAAN

0   25
MILES

Lingayen
Gulf

JAN 45

LUZON

MINDORO

DEC 44

APR 45

SAMAR

PANAY

OCT 44

—10°

PALAWAN

FEB 45

MAR 45

Cebu

LEYTE

10°

NEGROS

Bohol

MAR 45

SULU

SEA

MINDANAO

MAR 45

APR 45

JUN 45

Brunei
Bay

NORTH
BORNEO

B

APR 45

SULU ARCHIPELAGO

JUL 45

Sarangani
Bay

MAY 45

THE PHILIPPINE AREA

0   100   200   300
STATUTE MILES

125°

Morotai

MAP 5

area. Within this area the natural goal of the Southwest Pacific drive was the Philippines, but that of the Central Pacific drive could be either the Philippines or Formosa. As the drives along the two lines got under way in earnest in 1944, the choice between the two became the central strategic issue.

Cartwheel: The Encirclement of Rabaul

In June 1943 MacArthur and Halsey resumed their offensive to reduce the Japanese stronghold at Rabaul — a prerequisite to further advances along the Southwest Pacific axis toward the Philippines. The plan for the campaign provided for a carefully phased series of operations in each theater, each designed to secure a strategic position where air cover could be provided for further advances. The first of the series started in late June when MacArthur landed American troops on the Woodlark and Kiriwina Islands off eastern New Guinea and at Nassau Bay on the New Guinea coast, and Halsey's forces made their first landings on the New Georgia group in the Central Solomons. From these beginnings the operations proceeded up the ladder of the Solomons, along the coast of New Guinea, and across the straits to New Britain Island generally as scheduled, despite strong Japanese reaction.

In the Solomons by early August Army forces under Halsey had secured New Georgia with its important Munda airfield, but the campaign was not completed until October when U.S. and New Zealand troops occupied Vella Lavella, between New Georgia and Bougainville. At the end of October, New Zealanders and U.S. marines landed on Treasury and Choiseul Islands to secure bases for the assault on Bougainville; that assault got under way on November 1 when marines landed, followed soon after by the Army's 37th Division. In each phase of the Solomons campaign, the Japanese sought unsuccessfully to contest Allied air and naval supremacy, to land reinforcements, and to launch strong counterattacks against Allied beachheads, losing in the effort both planes and combat ships they could ill afford to spare. Air and naval losses suffered in the Solomons crippled the Japanese Fleet for months to come and helped to pave the way for the successful Central Pacific drive that got under way in November. With the repulse of the

124

Japanese counterattack on Bougainville, by the end of November security of the American beachhead on that island was assured, permitting the development of a major American air base. With the taking of Bougainville, the main part of the South Pacific Area's task in Operation CARTWHEEL was completed.

MacArthur's forces meanwhile continued their offensives, with Australian troops carrying most of the burden in New Guinea. In early September the U.S. Army's 503d Parachute Regiment, in the first airborne operation of the Pacific war, seized an airfield at Nadzab, inland from Lae and Salamaua. Australian troops cleared Lae and Salamaua by mid-September and, flown into Nadzab, moved on to the Huon peninsula. Elements of the U.S. 32d Division landed at the western end of the peninsula in January 1944 in an attempt to trap a large Japanese force, but by the time Australian and American units had sealed the western exits to the peninsula most of the Japanese had escaped northwest to Hansa Bay and Wewak.

In the meantime, MacArthur and Halsey had assembled the forces to launch a final offensive toward Rabaul, but the Joint Chiefs decided that the actual seizure of that objective would be too costly in terms of men, equipment, and time. They preferred to encircle Rabaul, neutralize it by air bombardment, and push on to seize an offensive base farther west, in the Admiralty Islands. A new series of operations toward these ends started in MacArthur's theater on December 15, 1943, when U.S. Army units landed on the south coast of western New Britain, and on the 26th, the 1st Marine Division landed on the north coast. In mid-February 1944 New Zealand troops of the South Pacific Area secured an air base site on Green Island, north of Rabaul, and on the last day of the month MacArthur began landing the 1st Cavalry Division (an infantry unit retaining its former designation) on the Admiralties, closing the western and northwestern approaches to Rabaul. Marines under Halsey seized a final air base site on Emiau, north of Rabaul, on March 20, while Marine and Army units under MacArthur secured additional positions in western and central New Britain from March to May 1944. The major Japanese base at Rabaul, with its 100,000-man garrison, was as effectively out of the war as if it had been destroyed. In the process of encircling Rabaul, the Allies had also left to wither on the vine another important Japanese base at Kavieng on New Ireland, north of Rabaul.

In the last phase of the campaign against Rabaul, a pattern developed that came to characterize much of the war in the Pacific. The Allies would mount no frontal attacks against strongly entrenched Japanese forces if they could avoid it; they would not advance island by island across a vast ocean studded with myriad atolls and island groups. Rather, they would advance in great bounds, limited only by the range of land-based air cover or the availability of carrier-based air support. The Allies would deceive and surprise the Japanese; they would bypass major strongpoints and leave them reduced to strategic and tactical impotence.

The Central Pacific Drive Begins

The necessity for relying primarily on support of land-based aircraft curtailed the length of the jumps in the South and Southwest Pacific in 1943. The Navy's limited supply of aircraft carriers could not be employed to best advantage in the narrow waters around New Guinea and the Solomons. By mid-1943, however, new larger and faster carriers of the *Essex* class (27,000 tons) and lighter carriers of the *Independence* class (11,000 tons) were joining the Pacific Fleet. Around these new carriers Admiral Nimitz built naval task forces tailored in each case to the particular operation at hand. The task forces consisted of a mix of carriers, destroyers, cruisers, battleships, submarines, minesweepers, and support craft. In the broad expanses of the Central Pacific, these air carrier task forces could provide both air and naval support for far longer leaps forward, while the entire Pacific Fleet stood ready to confront the main Japanese Fleet at any time it chose to give battle.

The Central Pacific drive got under way on November 20, 1943, when Nimitz sent Army and Marine forces to the Gilbert Islands to seize bases from which to support subsequent jumps into the Marshalls. Troops and supplies for the Gilberts loaded at Hawaii on newly developed assault shipping and sailed more than 2,000 miles to be set ashore by specially designed landing craft and amphibian vehicles. Makin, the Army objective, fell to the 27th

Division after four days of hard fighting. Tarawa, where the 2d Marine Division went ashore, proved a bloody affair that provided a stiff test for American amphibious doctrine, techniques, and equipment. Naval gunfire vessels and carrier-based aircraft provided support during and after the assault.

The advance to the Gilberts disclosed that U.S. forces had not entirely mastered certain aspects of amphibious warfare, especially naval gunfire support, co-ordination of air support, and ship-to-shore communications. But valuable lessons were learned that, added to the earlier experiences of the South and Southwest Pacific Areas, established a pattern of island warfare which represented one of the major tactical developments of the war. First, air and naval forces isolated an objective and softened its defenses; simultaneously, joint forces would attack or feint toward other islands to deceive the Japanese. The approach of convoys carrying the ground assault forces to the main objective signaled the opening of final, intensive air and naval bombardment of the landing beaches. Whenever practicable, small forces occupied neighboring islands as sites for land-based artillery. Under cover of all these supporting fires, the landing forces moved from ship to shore in echelons, or waves, rocket-firing landing craft in the lead and amphibian tanks and tractors following to carry the assault troops directly onto the beaches and inland. Finally came landing craft with more infantry and with tanks, artillery, and supporting troops. Supplies followed rapidly as the assault forces secured and expanded the beachhead. Amphibious techniques were refined and modified to some extent after the Gilberts, but the lessons learned there made it unnecessary to effect any radical changes in amphibious doctrine throughout the rest of the war.

The Japanese did not react strongly to the loss of the Gilberts, and at the end of January 1944 Nimitz' Army and Marine forces moved into the eastern and central Marshalls to seize Majuro and Kwajalein. The strength employed in this operation proved so preponderant and Japanese defenses so weak that Nimitz was able to accelerate his next advance by two and a half months, and on February 17 landed Marine and Army units on Eniwetok Atoll in the western Marshalls. Concurrently, he conducted a long-awaited carrier strike against Truk in the central Carolines, considered Japan's key bastion in the Central Pacific. The raid revealed that the Japanese had virtually abandoned Truk as a naval base, and the capture of the atoll, set for June, no longer appeared necessary. Nimitz then drew up plans to invade the Marianas in mid-June and move on to the western Carolines and Palaus in mid-September, again accelerating the pace of the advance.

Acceleration of the Pacific Drive

General MacArthur had also pushed forward the Southwest Pacific Area's timetable. Having landed in the Admiralties a month ahead of his original schedule, he proposed to cancel operations against Hansa Bay and Wewak on the northeast coast of New Guinea in favor of a jump to Hollandia and Aitape, on the north-central coast, in April, two months earlier than previously planned. He would then continue northwestward along the coast in a campaign entailing the steady extension of land-based air cover by the seizure of successive air base sites until he reached the Vogelkop, at the eastern end of New Guinea, and then proceed to Mindanao, southernmost of the Philippine Islands.

The Joint Chiefs, quickly seizing the fruits of their strategy of opportunism, on March 12, 1944, rearranged the schedule of major Pacific operations. They provided for the assault by MacArthur's forces on Hollandia and Aitape in April with the support of a carrier task force from the Pacific Fleet, to be followed by Nimitz's move into the Marianas in June and into the Palaus in September. While Nimitz was employing the major units of the Pacific Fleet in these ventures, MacArthur was to continue his advance along the New Guinea coast with the forces at his disposal. In November, he was again to have the support of main units of the Pacific Fleet in an assault on Mindanao. Refusing yet to make a positive choice of what was to follow, the Joint Chiefs directed MacArthur to plan for the invasion of Luzon and Nimitz to plan for the invasion of Formosa early in 1945.

The March 12 directive served as a blueprint for an accelerated drive in the Pacific in the spring and summer of 1944. On April 22 Army forces under MacArthur landed at Hollandia and Aitape. At neither place was the issue ever in doubt, although during July the Japanese who had been bypassed at Wewak launched an abortive counterattack against Aitape. Protected by land-based aircraft from Hollandia, MacArthur's Army units next jumped 125 miles northwest on May 17 to seize another air base site at Wakde Island, landing first on the New Guinea mainland opposite the chief objective. A ground campaign of about a month and a half ensued against a Japanese division on the mainland, but, without waiting for the outcome of the fight, other Army troops carried the advance northwestward on May 27 another 180 miles to Biak Island.

At this point the wisdom of conducting twin drives across the Pacific emerged. The Japanese Navy was preparing for a showdown battle it expected to develop off the Marianas in June. MacArthur's move to Biak put land-based planes in position to keep under surveillance and to harry the Japanese Fleet, which was assembling in Philippine waters before moving into the Central Pacific. Reckoning an American-controlled Biak an unacceptable threat to their flank, the Japanese risked major elements of their fleet to send strong reinforcements to Biak in an attempt to drive MacArthur's forces off the island. They also deployed to bases within range of Biak about half their land-based air strength from the Marianas, Carolines, and Palaus — planes upon which their fleet depended for support during the forthcoming battle off the Marianas.

After two partially successful attempts to reinforce Biak, the Japanese assembled for a third try enough naval strength to overwhelm local American naval units; but just as the formidable force was moving toward Biak the Japanese learned the U.S. Pacific Fleet was off the Marianas. They hastily assembled their naval forces and sailed northwestward for the engagement known as the Battle of the Philippine Sea. Having lost their chance to surprise the U.S. Navy, handicapped by belated deployment, and deprived of anticipated land-based air support, the Japanese suffered another shattering naval defeat. This defeat, which assured the success of the invasions of both Biak and the Marianas, illustrates well the interdependence of operations in the two Pacific areas. It also again demonstrated that the U.S. Pacific Fleet's carrier task forces were the decisive element in the Pacific war.

Army and Marine divisions under Nimitz landed on Saipan in the Marianas on June 15, 1944, to begin a bloody three-week battle for control of the island. Next, on July 21, Army and Marine units invaded Guam, 100 miles south of Saipan, and three days later marines moved on to Tinian Island. An important turning point of the Pacific war, the American seizure of the Marianas brought the Japanese home islands within reach of the U.S. Army Air Forces' B-29 bombers, which in late November began to fly missions against the Japanese homeland.

At Biak Japanese resistance delayed capture of the best airfield sites until late June. On July 2, MacArthur's Army forces moved on to Noemfoor Island, ninety miles to the west, in a combined parachute-amphibious operation designed to broaden the base of the Southwest Pacific's air deployment. On July 30 the 6th Division continued on to the northwestern tip of New Guinea to secure another air base, and on September 15 MacArthur landed the reinforced 31st Division on Morotai Island, between New Guinea and Mindanao in the Philippines. On the same day Nimitz sent the 1st Marine Division ashore on Peleliu in the southern Palaus, and on the 17th the 81st Division from Nimitz' command landed on Angaur, just south of Peleliu. A regimental combat team of the 81st Division secured Ulithi Atoll, midway between Peleliu and the Marianas, without opposition on September 23.

With these landings the approach to the Philippines was virtually completed. The occupation of Morotai proved easy, and the island provided airfields for the support of advances into the Philippines and Indies. The Pacific Fleet employed Ulithi as a forward anchorage. Hard fighting dragged on in the Palaus through November, but as the result of another acceleration in the pace of Pacific operations these islands never played the role originally planned for them.

In twin drives, illustrative of the principles of maneuver, objective, economy of force, surprise, and mass, the Allied forces of the Pacific had arrived in mid-September 1944 at the threshold of their strategic objective, the Luzon-Formosa-China coast triangle. In seven months MacArthur's forces had moved forward nearly 1,500 miles from the Admiralties to Morotai; in ten months Nimitz' forces had advanced over 4,500 miles from Hawaii to the Palaus. The time had now arrived when a final choice had to be made of the main objective in the target area.

The Decision to Invade Luzon

During the summer of 1944, as the battles raged along both lines of advance, the strategic debate over the choice of Luzon versus Formosa also waxed hot. General MacArthur argued fervently that the proper course was to move through the Philippines to Luzon, cutting the Japanese lines of communications southward, establishing a base for bombardment and invasion of Japan, and fulfilling a solemn national obligation to liberate the Philippine people. Admiral Ernest J. King, Chief of Naval Operations, just as adamantly insisted that the war could be shortened by directing the Pacific advance from the Marianas and Palaus toward Formosa, the China coast, and Japan proper, seizing only the essential positions in the southern and central Philippines necessary to render air support for these advances. The arguments for Formosa were cogent enough. Its strategic position made it a better island steppingstone to the China coast or the Japanese home islands, a position from which Japanese communications to the south could be cut more effectively than from Luzon, and a closer-in position from which to conduct strategic bombardment. But it also could prove to be a more difficult position to take, and Nimitz did not have in his theater sufficient Army supporting and service troops, without reinforcement, to sustain a land campaign on the island. It might be difficult, too, to mount an invasion of Formosa as long as the Japanese could, from strong positions on Luzon, interfere with the Allied line of communications. Another consideration involved the real value of a foothold on the China coast. By the early fall of 1944, air base sites in east China from which the Allies had hoped to support Pacific operations and bomb Japan appeared irretrievably lost, and the Marianas already provided bases for the B-29's almost as close to Tokyo as Formosa. The need to seize and develop a port on the China coast thus lost much of its urgency, and the argument that Formosa was the best steppingstone to China became less compelling. Then, too, a successful invasion of either Luzon or Formosa required some concentration of forces from the two theaters. It was far easier to shift highly mobile naval resources in Nimitz' theater to the Philippines than it was to redeploy Army troops from the

Southwest Pacific to support Nimitz' invasion of Formosa and the jump to the China coast with which he hoped to follow it.

At the time of the Morotai and Palaus landings, MacArthur's plans for invasion of the Philippines called for a preliminary assault in southern Mindanao on November 15, 1944, to secure air bases for the support of a larger attack at Leyte, in the east-central Philippines, on December 20. He would follow this with a large-scale assault on Lingayen Gulf in February 1945. Nimitz meanwhile planned to mount an invasion of Yap in the Carolines in October 1944 and then would prepare to launch his attack on Formosa as soon afterward as the elements of the Pacific Fleet required for operations in the southern and central Philippines could be returned. Obviously, there had to be a choice between Luzon and Formosa, for the Pacific Fleet would be required to support either operation.

The course of events went far to dictate the final choice. In mid-September Admiral Halsey's carrier task forces providing strategic support for the Morotai and Palaus operations struck the central and southern Philippines. Halsey found Japanese air strength unexpectedly weak and uncovered few signs of significant ground or naval activity. On the basis of Halsey's reports, MacArthur and Nimitz proposed to the Joint Chiefs a move directly to Leyte in October, bypassing Mindanao. Nimitz agreed to divert to the Leyte invasion the 3-division corps then mounting out of Hawaii for the assault against Yap. The Joint Chiefs quickly approved the new plan, and the decision to invade Leyte two months ahead of schedule gave MacArthur's arguments to move onto Luzon almost irresistible force. MacArthur now reported that he could undertake the invasion of Luzon in December 1944, whereas all the planners' estimates indicated that resources for an invasion of Formosa — particularly service troops and shipping — could not be readied before February 1945 at the earliest. Nimitz proposed to shift the Central Pacific attack northward against Iwo Jima in the Bonins in January 1945 and then against Okinawa and other islands in the Ryukyus early in March. On October 3, Admiral King bowing to the inevitable, accepted the new plans and the Joint Chiefs issued directives to MacArthur for the invasion of Luzon on December 20 and to Nimitz for the invasion of Iwo Jima and Okinawa early in 1945.

UNLOADING SUPPLIES ON A LEYTE BEACH

Pacific strategy had been cast into almost its final mold. In the end, the China coast objective disappeared entirely from planning boards. Final plans for the defeat of Japan envisaged gradual tightening of the ring by blockade and bombardment from the Marianas, Philippines, and Ryukyus with an invasion of the home islands to be mounted from these bases.

The Philippines Campaign

The main assault at Leyte took place on October 20, 1944, as four Army divisions landed abreast in the largest amphibious operation yet conducted in the Pacific. Vice Adm. Thomas C. Kinkaid, MacArthur's naval commander, controlled the amphibious phases, including naval gunfire support and close air support by planes based on escort carriers. Ground forces were under Lt. Gen. Walter Krueger, commanding the U.S. Sixth Army; land-based air forces of the Southwest Pacific Area in general support were commanded by Lt. Gen. George C. Kenney. MacArthur himself exercised unified command over the air, ground, and naval commanders. The fast carrier task forces of the Pacific Fleet, providing strategic support, operated under the control of Admiral Halsey, who reported to Nimitz, not MacArthur. There was no provision for unified naval command, and Halsey's orders were such that he could make his principal mission the destruction of the Japanese Fleet rather than the support of MacArthur's entry into the Philippines.

The Japanese had originally planned to make their stand in the Philippines on Luzon, but the invasion of Leyte moved them to reconsider, since they now decided that the entire Philippine Archipelago would be strategically lost if the U.S. Army secured a foothold in the central islands. They therefore began sending ground reinforcements to Leyte; increased their land-based air strength in the Philippines in the hope of destroying Allied shipping in Leyte Gulf and maintaining local air superiority; and dispatched their remaining naval strength to Leyte Gulf to destroy Kinkaid's invasion fleet and to block Allied access to the Philippines. The ensuing air-naval Battle of Leyte Gulf was the most critical moment of the campaign, and proved one of the most decisive actions of the Pacific war.

Admiral Halsey, without consulting MacArthur or Kinkaid, pulled the bulk of his carrier forces northward to intercept part of the Japanese Fleet, leaving Leyte Gulf open to other Japanese Fleet units. Gallant, desperate action by Kinkaid's old battleships and escort carrier planes turned back the Japanese in the gulf, assuring the safety of the landing forces. It had been a close thing, clearly demonstrating the dangers of divided command. In the end, however, the combined operations of Kinkaid's and Halsey's forces virtually eliminated the Japanese Navy as a factor in the Pacific war.

With the Leyte beaches secure, U.S. Army units proceeded to destroy the Japanese ground forces. Miserable weather bogged down the pace of operations, made supply difficult, delayed airfield construction, curtailed air support, and permitted the Japanese to continue to ship reinforcements to the island. The reinforcement program came to a sudden halt in December when the 77th Division executed an amphibious envelopment on Leyte's west coast, and by late December the Sixth Army had secured the most important sections of the island, those required for air and logistical bases. Japanese troops in the mountains of northwestern Leyte continued organized resistance well into the spring of 1945, occupying the

GENERAL MACARTHUR AND MEMBERS OF HIS STAFF WADING ASHORE AT LEYTE

energies of large portions of Lt. Gen. Robert L. Eichelberger's newly formed Eighth Army.

While the fight on Leyte continued, MacArthur's forces moved on to Luzon only slightly behind schedule. The first step of the Luzon Campaign was the seizure of an air base in southwestern Mindoro, 150 miles south of Manila, on December 15, 1944, two Army regiments accomplishing the task with ease. The invasion of Luzon itself started on January 9, 1945, when four Army divisions landed along the shores of Lingayen Gulf. Command arrangements were similar to those at Leyte, and again fast carrier task forces under Halsey operated in general support and not under MacArthur's control. Within three days five Army divisions, a separate regimental combat team, two artillery groups, an armored group, and supporting service units were ashore and had begun a drive down the Central Plains of Luzon toward Manila. The Japanese were incapable of naval intervention at Lingayen Gulf, and their most significant reaction was to throw a number of kamikaze (suicide plane) attacks against Kinkaid's naval forces for four days.

135

General Tomoyuki Yamashita, commanding Japanese forces in the Philippines, did not intend to defend the Central Plains-Manila Bay region, the strategic prize of Luzon. Knowing he would receive no reinforcements and believing the issue in the Philippines had been decided at Leyte, he sought only to pin down major elements of MacArthur's forces in the hope of delaying Allied progress toward Japan. For this purpose he moved the bulk of his troops into mountain strongholds, where they could conduct a protracted, bloody defensive campaign. But Japanese naval forces on Luzon, only nominally under Yamashita, decided to ignore this concept in favor of defending Manila and Manila Bay. Thus, when U.S. Army units reached Manila on February 3, it took them a month of bitter building-to-building fighting to root out the Japanese. Meanwhile, operations to clear Manila Bay had begun with a minor amphibious landing at the southern tip of Bataan on February 15. The next day a combined parachute-amphibious assault, involving two Army regiments, initiated a battle to clear Corregidor Island. Other forces cleared additional islands in Manila Bay and secured the south shore. By mid-March the bay was open for Allied shipping, but an immense salvage and repair job was necessary before the Allies could fully exploit Manila's excellent port facilities.

The reinforced 38th Division had landed meanwhile near Subic Bay and had cut across the base of Bataan peninsula to prevent the Japanese from holing up on Bataan as had MacArthur's forces three years earlier. The 11th Airborne Division undertook both amphibious and parachute landings in southern Luzon to start clearing that region, and the 158th Regimental Combat Team made an amphibious assault in southeastern Luzon to secure the Bicol peninsula. Turning against the Japanese mountain strongholds, MacArthur continued to pour reinforcements onto Luzon, and the land campaign there ultimately evolved into the largest of the Pacific war. MacArthur committed to Luzon ten divisions, two regiments of another division, and three separate regimental combat teams. Guerrillas also played a large role. One guerrilla unit came to substitute for a regularly constituted division, and other guerrilla forces of battalion and regimental size supplemented the efforts of the Army units. Moreover, the loyal and willing Filipino population immeasurably eased the problems of supply, construction, and civil administration.

136

U. S. Paratroopers Dropping on Corregidor

Except for a strong pocket in the mountains of north central Luzon, organized Japanese resistance ended by late June 1945. The rugged terrain in the north, along with rainy weather, prevented Krueger's Sixth Army from applying its full strength to the reduction of this pocket. Eichelberger's Eighth Army took over responsibility for operations on Luzon at the end of June and continued the pressure against Yamashita's force in the last-stand area, but they held out there until the end of the war.

While Sixth Army was destroying Japanese forces on Luzon, Eighth Army ultimately employed five divisions, portions of a sixth division, a separate regimental combat team, and strong guerrilla units in its campaign to reconquer the southern Philippines. This effort began when a regimental combat team of the 41st Division

137

landed on Palawan Island on February 28, 1945. Here engineers built an air base from which to help cut Japan's line of communications to the south and to support later advances in the southern Philippines and the Indies. On March 10, another regimental combat team of the 41st, later reinforced, landed near Zamboanga in southwestern Mindanao, and soon thereafter Army units began moving southwest toward Borneo along the Sulu Archipelago. In rapid succession Eighth Army units then landed on Panay, Cebu, northwestern Negros, Bohol, central Mindanao, southeastern Negros, northern Mindanao, and finally at Sarangani Bay in southern Mindanao, once intended as the first point of re-entry into the Philippines. At some locales bitter fighting raged for a time, but the issue was never in doubt and organized Japanese resistance in the southern Philippines had largely collapsed by the end of May. Mopping up continued to the end of the war, with reorganized and re-equipped guerrilla forces bearing much of the burden.

The last offensives in the Southwest Pacific Area started on May 1 when an Australian brigade went ashore on Tarakan Island, Borneo. Carried to the beaches by landing craft manned by U.S. Army engineers, the Australians had air support from fields on Morotai and in the southern Philippines. On June 10 an Australian division landed at Brunei Bay, Borneo, and another Australian division went ashore at Balikpapan on July 1 in what proved to be the final amphibious assault of the war.

Iwo Jima and Okinawa

Since slow-base development at Leyte had forced MacArthur to delay the Luzon invasion from December to January, Nimitz in turn had to postpone his target dates for the Iwo Jima and Okinawa operations, primarily because the bulk of the naval resources in the Pacific — fast carrier task forces, escort carrier groups, assault shipping, naval gunfire support vessels, and amphibious assault craft — had to be shifted between the two theaters for major operations. The alteration of schedules again illustrated the interdependence of the Southwest and Central Pacific Areas.

The Iwo Jima assault finally took place on February 19, 1945, with the 4th and 5th Marine Divisions, supported by minor Army elements, making the landings. The 3d Marine Division reinforced the assault, and an Army regiment ultimately took over as island garrison. The marines had to overcome fanatic resistance from firmly entrenched Japanese, who held what was probably the strongest defensive system American forces encountered during the Pacific war, and it took a month of bloody fighting to secure the island. In early March a few crippled B-29's made emergency landings on Iwo; by the end of the month an airfield was fully operational for fighter planes. Later, engineers constructed a heavy bomber field and another fighter base on the island.

The invasion of the Ryukyus began on March 26 when the 77th Division landed on the Kerama Islands, fifteen miles west of Okinawa, to secure a forward naval base, a task traditionally assigned to marines. On April 1 the 7th and 96th Divisions and the 2d and 6th Marine Divisions executed the assault on the main objective, Okinawa. Two more Army divisions and a Marine infantry regiment later reinforced it. Another amphibious assault took place on April 16, when the 77th Division seized Ie Shima, four miles west of Okinawa, and the final landing in the Ryukyus came on June 26, when a small force of marines went ashore on Kume Island, fifty miles west of Okinawa. Ground forces at Okinawa were first under the U.S. Tenth Army, Lt. Gen. Simon B. Buckner commanding. When General Buckner was killed on June 18, Marine Lt. Gen. Roy S. Geiger took over until General Joseph W. Stilwell assumed command on the 23d.

The Japanese made no attempt to defend the Okinawa beaches, but instead fell back to prepared cave and tunnel defenses on inland hills. Bitterly defending every inch of ground, the Japanese continued organized resistance until late June. Meanwhile, Japanese suicide planes had inflicted extensive damage on Nimitz' naval forces, sinking about 25 ships and damaging nearly 165 more in an unsuccessful attempt to drive Allied naval power from the western Pacific. Skillful small unit tactics, combined with great concentrations of naval, air, and artillery bombardment, turned the tide of the ground battle on Okinawa itself. Especially noteworthy was the close support that naval gunfire vessels provided the ground forces and the close air support furnished by Army, Navy, and Marine aircraft.

Capture of Okinawa and other positions in the Ryukyus gave the

139

Allies both air and naval bases within easy striking distance of Japan. By early May fighter planes from Okinawa had begun flights over Japan, and as rapidly as fields became available bombers, including units from the Southwest Pacific Area, came forward to mount attacks in preparation for the invasion of the home islands. The forward anchorages in the Ryukyus permitted the Pacific Fleet to keep in almost continuous action against Japanese targets. The Ryukyus campaign had brought Allied forces in the Pacific to Japan's doorstep.

The American Effort in China, Burma, and India

While American forces in the Pacific, under the unified direction of the U.S. Joint Chiefs of Staff, made spectacular advances, the Allied effort in Southeast Asia bogged down in a mire of conflicting national purposes. The hopes Americans held, in the early stages of the war, that Chinese manpower and bases would play a vitally important role in the defeat of Japan were doomed to disappointment. Americans sought to achieve great aims on the Asiatic mainland at small cost, looking to the British in India and the Chinese, with their vast reservoirs of manpower, to carry the main burden of ground conflict. Neither proved capable of exerting the effort the Americans expected of them.

Early in 1942 the United States had sent General Stilwell to the Far East to command American forces in China, Burma, and India and to serve as Chief of Staff and principal adviser to Chiang Kai-shek, the leader of Nationalist China and Allied commander of the China theater. Stilwell's stated mission was "to assist in improving the efficiency of the Chinese Army." The Japanese conquest of Burma, cutting the last overland supply route to China, frustrated Stilwell's designs, for it left a long and difficult airlift from Assam to Kunming over the high peaks of the Himalayas as the only remaining avenue for the flow of supplies. The Americans assumed responsibility for the airlift, but its development was slow, hampered by a scarcity of transport planes, airfields, and trained pilots. Not until late in 1943 did it reach a monthly capacity of 10,000 tons, and in the intervening months few supplies flowed into China. The economy of the country continually tottered on the

140

brink of collapse, and the Chinese Army, although it was a massive force on paper, remained ill organized, ill equipped, poorly led, and generally incapable of offensive action.

Stilwell thought that the only solution was to retake Burma and reopen the land supply line to China, and this became the position of the U.S. Joint Chiefs of Staff. To achieve the goal Stilwell undertook the training and equipping of a Chinese force in India that eventually consisted of three divisions, and sought to concentrate a much larger force in Yunnan Province in China and to give it offensive capability. With these two Chinese forces he hoped to form a junction in north Burma, thus re-establishing land communications between China and India. Stilwell's scheme became part of the larger plan, ANAKIM, that had been approved by the Combined Chiefs of Staff at the Casablanca Conference. Neither the British nor the Chinese, however, had any real enthusiasm for ANAKIM, and in retrospect it seems clear that its execution in 1943 was beyond the capabilities of forces in the theater. Moreover, Chiang was quite dilatory in concentrating a force in Yunnan; Maj. Gen. Claire L. Chennault, commanding the small American air force in China, urged that the Hump air line should be used to support an air effort in China, rather than to supply Chinese ground forces. Chennault promised amazing results at small cost, and his proposals attracted President Roosevelt as well as the British and the Chinese. As an upshot, at the TRIDENT Conference in May 1943, the amphibious operation against Rangoon was canceled and a new plan for operations emerged that stressed Chennault's air operations and provided for a lesser ground offensive in central and northern Burma. Under this concept a new road would be built from Ledo in Assam Province, India, to join with the trace of the old Burma Road inside China. The Americans assumed responsibility for building the Ledo Road in the rear of Chinese forces advancing from India into Burma.

Logistical difficulties in India, however, again delayed the opening of any land offensive and kept the airlift well below target figures. Until the supply line north from Calcutta to the British and Chinese fronts could be improved — and this job took well over a year — both air and ground operations against the Japanese in Burma were handicapped. In October 1943 Chinese troops under Stilwell did start to clear northern Burma, and in the spring of 1944

141

a U.S. Army unit of regimental size, Merrill's Marauders, spearheaded new offensives to secure the trace for the overland road. But Myitkyina, the key point in the Japanese defenses in north Burma, did not fall until August 2 and by that time the effort in Burma had been relegated to a subsidiary role.

After the SEXTANT Conference in late 1943, in fact, the American staff no longer regarded it as probable that the overland route to China could be opened in time to permit Chinese forces to drive to the coast by the time American forces advancing across the Pacific reached there. While the Americans insisted on continuing the effort to open the Ledo Road, they now gave first priority to an air effort in China in support of the Pacific campaigns. The Army Air Forces, in May 1944, started to deploy the first of its B-29 groups to airfields in East China to commence bombing of strategic targets in Korea, Manchuria, and Japan. At the same time, Chennault's Fourteenth Air Force was directed to stockpile supplies for missions in support of Pacific forces as they neared the China coast. Again these projects proved to be more than could be supported over the Hump air line, particularly since transports had also to be used to supply the ground effort of both British and Chinese forces. Then the Japanese reacted strongly to the increased air effort and launched a ground offensive that overran most of the existing fields and proposed air base sites in east China. Both air and ground resources inside China had to be diverted to oppose the Japanese advance. The B-29's were removed to India in January 1945, and two months later were sent to Saipan where the major strategic bombing offensive against Japan was by that time being mounted. In sum, the air effort in China without the protection of an efficient Chinese Army fulfilled few of the goals proclaimed for it.

To meet the crisis in east China, President Roosevelt urged Chiang to place his U.S. supported armies under the command of General Stilwell; Chiang eventually refused and asked for Stilwell's recall, a request the President honored. In September 1944, Maj. Gen. Albert C. Wedemeyer replaced Stilwell as Chief of Staff to Chiang and commander of American forces in the China Theater; a separate theater in India and Burma was created with Lt. Gen. Dan I. Sultan as its commanding general. The command issue was dropped and the American strategy in China became simply one of trying to realize at least something from previous investments without additional commitments.

Ironically enough, it was in this phase, after the Pacific advances had outrun those in Southeast Asia, that objects of the 1942 strategy were realized, in large part because the Japanese, hard-pressed everywhere, were no longer able to support their forces in Burma and China adequately. British and Chinese forces advanced rapidly into Burma in the fall of 1944, and, on January 27, 1945, the junction between Chinese forces advancing from India and Yunnan finally took place, securing the trace of the Ledo Road. To the south, the British completed the conquest of central Burma and entered Rangoon from the north early in May. The land route to China was thus finally secured on all sides, but the Americans had already decided that they would develop the Ledo Road only as a one-way highway, though they did expand the airlift to the point where, in July 1945, it carried 74,000 tons into China.

With increased American supply support, Wedemeyer was able to make more progress in equipping and training the Chinese Army. Under his tutelage the Chinese were able to halt the Japanese advance at Chihchiang in April 1945, and, as the Japanese began to withdraw in order to prepare a citadel defense of their home islands, Wedemeyer and the Chinese laid plans to seize a port on the Chinese coast. The war came to an end, however, before this operation even started and before the training and equipping of a Chinese Army was anywhere near completion. Chiang's forces commenced the reoccupation of their homeland still, for the most part, ill equipped, ill organized, and poorly led.

The Japanese Surrender

During the summer of 1945, Allied forces in the Pacific had stepped up the pace of their air and naval attacks against Japan. In June and July carrier-based planes of the U.S. Pacific Fleet and U.S. Army Air Forces planes from the Marianas, Iwo Jima, and Okinawa struck the Japanese home islands continuously. During July Pacific Fleet surface units bombarded Japan's east coast, and in the same month a British carrier task force joined in the attack. Planes from the Philippines hit Japanese shipping in the South

143

China Sea and extended their strikes as far as Formosa and targets along the South China coast. American submarines redoubled their efforts to sweep Japanese shipping from the sea and sever the shipping lanes from Japan to the Indies and Southeast Asia. Throughout the war, in fact, submarines had preyed on Japanese merchant and combat vessels, playing a major role in isolating Japan from its conquests and thereby drastically reducing Japan's ability to wage war.

After Germany's surrender in May the United States embarked upon a huge logistical effort to redeploy more than a million troops from Europe, the United States, and other inactive theaters to the Pacific. The aim was to complete the redeployment in time to launch an invasion of Japan on November 1, and the task had to be undertaken in the face of competing shipping demands for demobilization of long-service troops, British redeployment, and civil relief in Europe. By the time the war ended, some 150,000 men had moved directly from Europe to the Pacific, but a larger transfer from the United States across the Pacific had scarcely begun. In the Pacific, MacArthur and Nimitz had been sparing no effort to expand ports and ready bases to receive the expected influx and to mount invasion forces. The two commanders were also completing plans for the invasion of Japan. In the last stage of the war, as all forces converged on Japan, the area unified commands were replaced by an arrangement that made MacArthur commander of all Army forces in the Pacific and Nimitz commander of all Navy forces.

By midsummer of 1945 most responsible leaders in Japan realized that the end was near. In June, those favoring peace had come out in the open, and Japan had already dispatched peace feelers through the Soviet Union, a country it feared might also be about to enter the war despite the existence of a non-aggression treaty between the two nations. As early as the Tehran Conference in late 1943 Stalin had promised to enter the war against Japan, and it was agreed at Yalta in February 1945 that the USSR would do so three months after the defeat of Germany. At the Potsdam Conference in July 1945 the Soviet Union reaffirmed its agreement to declare war on Japan. At this conference the United States and Britain, with China joining in, issued the famed Potsdam Declaration calling upon Japan to surrender promptly, and about the same time Presi-

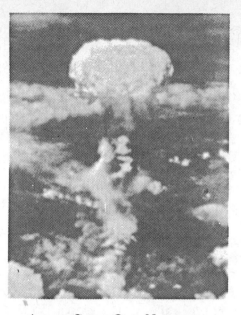

ATOMIC CLOUD OVER NAGASAKI

dent Truman decided to employ the newly tested atomic bomb against Japan in the event of continued Japanese resistance.

Despite the changing climate of opinion in Japan, the Japanese did not immediately accept the terms of the Potsdam Declaration. Accordingly, on August 6 a lone American B-29 from the Marianas dropped an atomic bomb on Hiroshima; on the 9th the Soviet Union came into the war and attacked Japanese forces in Manchuria; and on the same day another B-29 dropped a second atomic bomb on Nagasaki. The next day Japan sued for peace, and, with the signing of surrender terms aboard the USS *Missouri* in Tokyo Bay on September 2, the bitter global war came to an end.

Retrospect

In winning the Pacific war the Allies had found it unnecessary to press home their attacks and destroy the Japanese military forces except for the Japanese Fleet. By the end of the war Japan's Navy

145

had virtually ceased to exist; Japanese industry had been so hammered by air bombardment that Japan's ability to wage war was seriously reduced; and U.S. submarine and air actions had cut off sources of raw material. At the time of the surrender Japan still had 2,000,000 men under arms in the homeland and was capable of conducting a tenacious ground defense; about 3,000 Japanese aircraft were also operational. Nevertheless, the Japanese could hardly have continued the war for more than a few months. On the other hand, the fact that an invasion was not necessary certainly spared many American lives.

The great arbiter of the Pacific war had been American industrial power, which produced a mighty war machine. Out of this production had come the Pacific Fleet, a potent force that could overcome the vast reaches of the Pacific upon which the Japanese had depended so heavily as a defensive advantage. The decisive combat element of the fleet was the fast carrier task force, which carried the war deep into Japanese territory and supported advances far beyond the range of land-based aircraft. Land-based air power also played a decisive part. When carriers were not available to support offensives, it was land-based aviation that measured the distance of each forward move. Land-based aviation proved important as well in providing close support for ground operations, while aerial supply operations and troop movements contributed greatly to the success of the Allied campaigns.

Both naval and air forces were dependent upon shore bases, and the war in the Pacific demonstrated that even in a predominantly naval-air theater, ground combat forces are an essential part of the offensive team. The Japanese had also been dependent upon far-flung bases, so that much of the Allied effort during the war had gone into the seizure or neutralization of Japan's bases. Thus, the Pacific war was in large measure a war for bases. On the other hand, the U.S. Pacific Fleet, in one of the greatest logistical developments of the war, went far in the direction of carrying its bases with it by organizing fleet trains of support vessels that were capable of maintaining the fleet at sea over extended periods.

Another important facet of the Pacific war was the development and employment of amphibious assault techniques, repeatedly demonstrating the need for unified command. Air, ground, and naval teamwork, supremely important in the struggle against

Japan, occasionally broke down, but the success of the Allied campaigns illustrates that all three elements achieved it to a large degree. Strategic air bombardment in the Pacific, designed to cripple Japan's industrial capacity, did not get under way until well along in 1945. The damage inflicted on Japanese cities was enormous, but the effect, as in the case of the bomber offensive against Germany, remains unsettled, though the bombardment finally brought home to the Japanese people that the war was lost. The submarine played a vital role in reducing Japan's capabilities by taking a huge toll of Japanese shipping and by helping to cut Japan off from the resources of Southeast Asia.

In the final analysis Japan lost because the country did not have the means to fight a total war against the combination of industrial, air, naval, and human resources represented by the United States and its Allies. Admiral Isoroku Yamamoto, commander of the Japanese Fleet at the outbreak of the war, put his finger on the fatal weakness of the Japanese concept of the war, when he stated: "It is not enough that we should take Guam and the Philippines, or even Hawaii and San Francisco. We should have to march into Washington and sign the treaty in the White House." This the Japanese could never do, and because they could not they had to lose the war.

INDEX

Central Pacific drive, 126–130
　acceleration of, 128–130
Ceylon, 33
Chemical Warfare Service, 5, 32
Cherbourg, 99
Chiang Kai-shek, 140, 142, 143
China, 4, 12, 16, 30, 113–116, 121,
　122, 131
　American effort in, 140–143
　Lend-Lease aid to, 79
China-Burma-India theater, 30, 42,
　65, 72
Churchill, Winston, 21, 28–29, 30, 42,
　46, 48, 53, 57, 58, 59, 61, 62, 63, 79
Citizens' Military Training Camp
　(CMTC), 9, 10
Civilian Conservation Corps (CCC),
　11–12
Clark, Lt. Gen. Mark W., 92, 93, 94,
　112
Clark Field, 23
Combined Bomber Offensive, 54, 55
Combined Chiefs of Staff (CCS), 28–
　29, 77
Command and General Staff School, 6
Communications Zone, 104
Convoy system, 39–40
Coral Sea, Battle of the, 41, 45, 117
Corps of Engineers, 72
Corregidor Island, 136
Cotentin peninsula, 99
Crerar, Lt. Gen. Henry D. G., 101
Crete, 25
Cross-Channel Attack (Harrison), 59
Czech crisis of 1938, 15
Czechoslovakia, 16, 111

Demobilization, 2
Dempsey, Lt. Gen. Sir Miles C., 97
Denmark, 17
Devers, Lt. Gen. Jacob L., 103, 112
Dill, Field Marshal Sir John, 29
DUKW's (amphibious trucks), 91
Dunkerque, 19, 60

East Prussia, 109
Egypt, 25, 46, 47, 85
Eichelberger, Lt. Gen. Robert L., 135
Eighth Army, 94, 135, 138
VIII Corps, 107
81st Division, 130
82d Airborne Division, 99–100
Eisenhower, Dwight D., 10, 30, 43,
　45, 57, 61, 62, 63, 85, 86, 89, 90, 91,
　93, 94, 97, 99, 101–102, 103, 104–105,
　106, 110
El Alamein, 87
11th Airborne Division, 136
El Gazala, 46
Emiau (air base), 125
Engineer Service, 32
English Channel, 25, 43, 52, 55, 92,
　103–104

Enlisted Reserve Corps, 9
Espíritu Santo Island, 41
Essex (carrier), 126
Ethiopia, 13

Far East Air Force, 23, 116
1st Armored Division, 42
5th Marine Division, 138–139
Fifth Army, 92, 93, 94
V Corps, 107
Fiji Islands, 41
Finance Department, 5
1st Cavalry Division, 125
1st French Army, 103, 106
1st Marine Division, 119
First U.S. Army, 97, 101, 102, 103–104,
　106, 109–110
503d Parachute Regiment, 125
Foggia, 92
Formosa (Taiwan), 122, 128, 131, 132, 144
Fort Leavenworth, 6
Fortress Europe, 43
4th Marine Division, 100, 138–139
41st Division, 100, 137–138
43d Division, 120
France, 16, 17, 19, 56, 57, 58, 87,
　94, 111
　Allied build-up and breakout, 100–102
　Lend-Lease aid to, 79
　Normandy invasion, 95–100
　southern invasion of, 102–103
Fredendall, Maj. Gen. Lloyd R., 87–88
Free French Army, 85, 110
French Indochina, 34
French North Africa, 42, 47, 85

Geiger, Lt. Gen. Roy S., 139
General Headquarters (GHQ), 31
Germany, 3, 13, 17, 19, 24, 25, 28, 43, 44,
　47, 49, 71, 79, 92
　surrender of, 61, 62
Ghormley, Vice Adm. Robert L., 117
Gilbert Islands, 116, 122, 126
Good Neighbor policy, 13
Gothic Line, 94
Graves, Maj. Gen. William S., 3
Great Britain, 12, 16, 17, 19, 23, 25,
　26, 29, 38, 43, 60, 62, 78, 80, 95, 111
　Lend-Lease aid to, 79
Greater East Asia Co-Prosperity
　Sphere, 113–116
Greece, 25
Green Island, 125
Greenland, 21
Guadalcanal, 42, 117
　first U.S. offensives, 117–120
Guam, 33, 116, 130, 147
Gymnast project, 42

Halsey, Adm. William F., Jr., 30, 117, 120,
　124, 125, 132, 134
Hansa Bay, 125, 128
Harrison, Gordon, 59

150

153